ISBN-13: 978-0-9860455-2-3

Print number
10 9 8 7 6 5 4 3 2 1

TABLE OF CONTENTS

INTRODUCTION TO THE LSAT

The Law School Admission Test is a half-day standardized test required for admission to all ABA-approved law schools, most Canadian law schools, and many other law schools. It consists of five 35-minute sections of multiple-choice questions. Four of the five sections contribute to the test taker's score. These sections include one Reading Comprehension section, one Analytical Reasoning section, and two Logical Reasoning sections. The unscored section, commonly referred to as the variable section, typically is used to pretest new test questions or to preequate new test forms. The placement of this section in the LSAT will vary. A 35-minute writing sample is administered at the end of the test. The writing sample is not scored by LSAC, but copies are sent to all law schools to which you apply. The score scale for the LSAT is 120 to 180.

The LSAT is designed to measure skills considered essential for success in law school: the reading and comprehension of complex texts with accuracy and insight; the organization and management of information and the ability to draw reasonable inferences from it; the ability to think critically; and the analysis and evaluation of the reasoning and arguments of others.

The LSAT provides a standard measure of acquired reading and verbal reasoning skills that law schools can use as one of several factors in assessing applicants.

For up-to-date information about LSAC's services, go to our website, LSAC.org.

SCORING

Your LSAT score is based on the number of questions you answer correctly (the raw score). There is no deduction for incorrect answers, and all questions count equally. In other words, there is no penalty for guessing.

Test Score Accuracy—Reliability and Standard Error of Measurement

Candidates perform at different levels on different occasions for reasons quite unrelated to the characteristics of a test itself. The accuracy of test scores is best described by the use of two related statistical terms: reliability and standard error of measurement.

Reliability is a measure of how consistently a test measures the skills being assessed. The higher the reliability coefficient for a test, the more certain we can be that test takers would get very similar scores if they took the test again.

LSAC reports an internal consistency measure of reliability for every test form. Reliability can vary from 0.00 to 1.00, and a test with no measurement error would have a reliability coefficient of 1.00 (never attained in practice). Reliability coefficients for past LSAT forms have ranged from .90 to .95, indicating a high degree of consistency for these tests. LSAC expects the reliability of the LSAT to continue to fall within the same range.

LSAC also reports the amount of measurement error associated with each test form, a concept known as the standard error of measurement (SEM). The SEM, which is usually about 2.6 points, indicates how close a test taker's observed score is likely to be to his or her true score. True scores are theoretical scores that would be obtained from perfectly reliable tests with no measurement error—scores never known in practice.

Score bands, or ranges of scores that contain a test taker's true score a certain percentage of the time, can be derived using the SEM. LSAT score bands are constructed by adding and subtracting the (rounded) SEM to and from an actual LSAT score (e.g., the LSAT score, plus or minus 3 points). Scores near 120 or 180 have asymmetrical bands. Score bands constructed in this manner will contain an individual's true score approximately 68 percent of the time.

Measurement error also must be taken into account when comparing LSAT scores of two test takers. It is likely that small differences in scores are due to measurement error rather than to meaningful differences in ability. The standard error of score differences provides some guidance as to the importance of differences between two scores. The standard error of score differences is approximately 1.4 times larger than the standard error of measurement for the individual scores.

Thus, a test score should be regarded as a useful but approximate measure of a test taker's abilities as measured by the test, not as an exact determination of his or her abilities. LSAC encourages law schools to examine the range of scores within the interval that probably contains the test taker's true score (e.g., the test taker's score band) rather than solely interpret the reported score alone.

Adjustments for Variation in Test Difficulty

All test forms of the LSAT reported on the same score scale are designed to measure the same abilities, but one test form may be slightly easier or more difficult than another. The scores from different test forms are made comparable through a statistical procedure known as equating. As a result of equating, a given scaled score earned on different test forms reflects the same level of ability.

Research on the LSAT

Summaries of LSAT validity studies and other LSAT research can be found in member law school libraries and at LSAC.org.

To Inquire About Test Questions

If you find what you believe to be an error or ambiguity in a test question that affects your response to the question, contact LSAC by e-mail: LSATTS@LSAC.org, or write to Law School Admission Council, Test Development Group, PO Box 40, Newtown, PA 18940-0040.

HOW THIS PREPTEST DIFFERS FROM AN ACTUAL LSAT

This PrepTest is made up of the scored sections and writing sample from the actual disclosed LSAT administered in June 2014. However, it does not contain the extra, variable section that is used to pretest new test items of one of the three multiple-choice question types. The three multiple-choice question types may be in a different order in an actual LSAT than in this PrepTest. This is because the order of these question types is intentionally varied for each administration of the test.

THE THREE LSAT MULTIPLE-CHOICE QUESTION TYPES

The multiple-choice questions that make up most of the LSAT reflect a broad range of academic disciplines and are intended to give no advantage to candidates from a particular academic background.

The five sections of the test contain three different question types. The following material presents a general discussion of the nature of each question type and some strategies that can be used in answering them.

Analytical Reasoning Questions

Analytical Reasoning questions are designed to assess the ability to consider a group of facts and rules, and, given those facts and rules, determine what could or must be true. The specific scenarios associated with these questions are usually unrelated to law, since they are intended to be accessible to a wide range of test takers. However, the skills tested parallel those involved in determining what could or must be the case given a set of regulations, the terms of a contract, or the facts of a legal case in relation to the law. In Analytical Reasoning questions, you are asked to reason deductively from a set of statements and rules or principles that describe relationships among persons, things, or events.

Analytical Reasoning questions appear in sets, with each set based on a single passage. The passage used for each set of questions describes common ordering relationships or grouping relationships, or a combination of both types of relationships. Examples include scheduling employees for work shifts, assigning instructors to class sections, ordering tasks according to priority, and distributing grants for projects.

Analytical Reasoning questions test a range of deductive reasoning skills. These include:

- Comprehending the basic structure of a set of relationships by determining a complete solution to the problem posed (for example, an acceptable seating arrangement of all six diplomats around a table)

- Reasoning with conditional ("if-then") statements and recognizing logically equivalent formulations of such statements

- Inferring what could be true or must be true from given facts and rules

- Inferring what could be true or must be true from given facts and rules together with new information in the form of an additional or substitute fact or rule

- Recognizing when two statements are logically equivalent in context by identifying a condition or rule that could replace one of the original conditions while still resulting in the same possible outcomes

Analytical Reasoning questions reflect the kinds of detailed analyses of relationships and sets of constraints that a law student must perform in legal problem solving. For example, an Analytical Reasoning passage might describe six diplomats being seated around a table, following certain rules of protocol as to who can sit where. You, the test taker, must answer questions about the logical implications of given and new information. For example, you may be asked who can sit between diplomats X and Y, or who cannot sit next to X if W sits next to Y. Similarly, if you were a student in law school, you might be asked to analyze a scenario involving a set of particular circumstances and a set of governing rules in the form of constitutional provisions, statutes, administrative codes, or prior rulings that have been upheld. You might then be asked to determine the legal options in the scenario: what is required given the scenario, what is permissible given the scenario, and what is prohibited given the scenario. Or you might be asked to develop a "theory" for the case: when faced with an incomplete set of facts about the case, you must fill in the picture based on what is implied by the facts that are known. The problem could be elaborated by the addition of new information or hypotheticals.

No formal training in logic is required to answer these questions correctly. Analytical Reasoning questions are intended to be answered using knowledge, skills, and reasoning ability generally expected of college students and graduates.

Suggested Approach

Some people may prefer to answer first those questions about a passage that seem less difficult and then those that seem more difficult. In general, it is best to finish one passage before starting on another, because much time can be lost in returning to a passage and reestablishing familiarity with its relationships. However, if you are having great difficulty on one particular set of questions and are spending too much time on them, it may be to your advantage to skip that set of questions and go on to the next passage, returning to the problematic set of questions after you have finished the other questions in the section.

Do not assume that because the conditions for a set of questions look long or complicated, the questions based on those conditions will be especially difficult.

Read the passage carefully. Careful reading and analysis are necessary to determine the exact nature of the relationships involved in an Analytical Reasoning passage. Some relationships are fixed (for example, P and R must always work on the same project). Other relationships are variable (for example, Q must be assigned to either team 1 or team 3). Some relationships that are not stated explicitly in the conditions are implied by and can be deduced from those that are stated (for example, if one condition about paintings in a display specifies that Painting K must be to the left of Painting Y, and another specifies that Painting W must be to the left of Painting K, then it can be deduced that Painting W must be to the left of Painting Y).

In reading the conditions, do not introduce unwarranted assumptions. For instance, in a set of questions establishing relationships of height and weight among the members of a team, do not assume that a person who is taller than another person must weigh more than that person. As another example, suppose a set involves ordering and a question in the set asks what must be true if both X and Y must be earlier than Z; in this case, do not assume that X must be earlier than Y merely because X is mentioned before Y. All the information needed to answer each question is provided in the passage and the question itself.

The conditions are designed to be as clear as possible. Do not interpret the conditions as if they were intended to trick you. For example, if a question asks how many people could be eligible to serve on a committee, consider only those people named in the passage unless directed otherwise. When in doubt, read the conditions in their most obvious sense. Remember, however, that the language in the conditions is intended to be read for precise meaning. It is essential to pay particular attention to words that describe or limit relationships, such as "only," "exactly," "never," "always," "must be," "cannot be," and the like.

The result of this careful reading will be a clear picture of the structure of the relationships involved, including the kinds of relationships permitted, the participants in the relationships, and the range of possible actions or attributes for these participants.

Keep in mind question independence. Each question should be considered separately from the other questions in its set. No information, except what is given in the original conditions, should be carried over from one question to another.

In some cases a question will simply ask for conclusions to be drawn from the conditions as originally given. Some questions may, however, add information to the original conditions or temporarily suspend or replace one of the original conditions for the purpose of that question only. For example, if Question 1 adds the supposition "if P is sitting at table 2 ...," this supposition should NOT be carried over to any other question in the set.

Consider highlighting text and using diagrams. Many people find it useful to underline key points in the passage and in each question. In addition, it may prove very helpful to draw a diagram to assist you in finding the solution to the problem.

In preparing for the test, you may wish to experiment with different types of diagrams. For a scheduling problem, a simple calendar-like diagram may be helpful. For a grouping problem, an array of labeled columns or rows may be useful.

Even though most people find diagrams to be very helpful, some people seldom use them, and for some individual questions no one will need a diagram. There is by no means universal agreement on which kind of diagram is best for which problem or in which cases a diagram is most useful. Do not be concerned if a particular problem in the test seems to be best approached without the use of a diagram.

Logical Reasoning Questions

Arguments are a fundamental part of the law, and analyzing arguments is a key element of legal analysis. Training in the law builds on a foundation of basic reasoning skills. Law students must draw on the skills of analyzing, evaluating, constructing, and refuting arguments. They need to be able to identify what information is relevant to an issue or argument and what impact further evidence might have. They need to be able to reconcile opposing positions and use arguments to persuade others.

Logical Reasoning questions evaluate the ability to analyze, critically evaluate, and complete arguments as they occur in ordinary language. The questions are based on short arguments drawn from a wide variety of sources, including newspapers, general interest magazines, scholarly publications, advertisements, and informal discourse. These arguments mirror legal reasoning in the types of arguments presented and in their complexity, though few of the arguments actually have law as a subject matter.

Each Logical Reasoning question requires you to read and comprehend a short passage, then answer one question (or, rarely, two questions) about it. The questions are designed to assess a wide range of skills involved in thinking critically, with an emphasis on skills that are central to legal reasoning.

These skills include:

- Recognizing the parts of an argument and their relationships

- Recognizing similarities and differences between patterns of reasoning

- Drawing well-supported conclusions

- Reasoning by analogy

- Recognizing misunderstandings or points of disagreement

- Determining how additional evidence affects an argument

- Detecting assumptions made by particular arguments

- Identifying and applying principles or rules

- Identifying flaws in arguments

- Identifying explanations

The questions do not presuppose specialized knowledge of logical terminology. For example, you will not be expected to know the meaning of specialized terms such as "ad hominem" or "syllogism." On the other hand, you will be expected to understand and critique the reasoning contained in arguments. This requires that you possess a university-level understanding of widely used concepts such as argument, premise, assumption, and conclusion.

Suggested Approach

Read each question carefully. Make sure that you understand the meaning of each part of the question. Make sure that you understand the meaning of each answer choice and the ways in which it may or may not relate to the question posed.

Do not pick a response simply because it is a true statement. Although true, it may not answer the question posed.

Answer each question on the basis of the information that is given, even if you do not agree with it. Work within the context provided by the passage. LSAT questions do not involve any tricks or hidden meanings.

Reading Comprehension Questions

Both law school and the practice of law revolve around extensive reading of highly varied, dense, argumentative, and expository texts (for example, cases, codes, contracts, briefs, decisions, evidence). This reading must be exacting, distinguishing precisely what is said from what is not said. It involves comparison, analysis, synthesis, and application (for example, of principles and rules). It involves drawing appropriate inferences and applying ideas and arguments to new contexts. Law school reading also requires the ability to grasp unfamiliar subject matter and the ability to penetrate difficult and challenging material.

The purpose of LSAT Reading Comprehension questions is to measure the ability to read, with understanding and insight, examples of lengthy and complex materials similar to those commonly encountered in law school. The Reading Comprehension section of the LSAT contains four sets of reading questions, each set consisting of a selection of reading material followed by five to eight questions. The reading selection in three of the four sets consists of a single reading passage; the other set contains two related shorter passages. Sets with two passages are a variant of Reading Comprehension called Comparative Reading, which was introduced in June 2007.

Comparative Reading questions concern the relationships between the two passages, such as those of generalization/instance, principle/application, or point/counterpoint. Law school work often requires reading two or more texts in conjunction with each other and understanding their relationships. For example, a law student may read a trial court decision together with an appellate court decision that overturns it, or identify the fact pattern from a hypothetical suit together with the potentially controlling case law.

Reading selections for LSAT Reading Comprehension questions are drawn from a wide range of subjects in the humanities, the social sciences, the biological and physical sciences, and areas related to the law. Generally, the selections are densely written, use high-level vocabulary, and contain sophisticated argument or complex rhetorical structure (for example, multiple points of view). Reading Comprehension questions require you to read carefully and accurately, to determine the relationships among the various parts of the reading selection, and to draw reasonable inferences from the material in the selection. The questions may ask about the following characteristics of a passage or pair of passages:

- The main idea or primary purpose

- Information that is explicitly stated

- Information or ideas that can be inferred

- The meaning or purpose of words or phrases as used in context

- The organization or structure

- The application of information in the selection to a new context

- Principles that function in the selection

- Analogies to claims or arguments in the selection

- An author's attitude as revealed in the tone of a passage or the language used

- The impact of new information on claims or arguments in the selection

Suggested Approach

Since reading selections are drawn from many different disciplines and sources, you should not be discouraged if you encounter material with which you are not familiar. It is important to remember that questions are to be answered exclusively on the basis of the information provided in the selection. There is no particular knowledge that you are expected to bring to the test, and you should not make inferences based on any prior knowledge of a subject that you may have. You may, however, wish to defer working on a set of questions that seems particularly difficult or unfamiliar until after you have dealt with sets you find easier.

Strategies. One question that often arises in connection with Reading Comprehension has to do with the most effective and efficient order in which to read the selections and questions. Possible approaches include:

- reading the selection very closely and then answering the questions;

- reading the questions first, reading the selection closely, and then returning to the questions; or

- skimming the selection and questions very quickly, then rereading the selection closely and answering the questions.

Test takers are different, and the best strategy for one might not be the best strategy for another. In preparing for the test, therefore, you might want to experiment with the different strategies and decide what works most effectively for you.

Remember that your strategy must be effective under timed conditions. For this reason, the first strategy—reading the selection very closely and then answering the questions—may be the most effective for you. Nonetheless, if you believe that one of the other strategies

might be more effective for you, you should try it out and assess your performance using it.

Reading the selection. Whatever strategy you choose, you should give the passage or pair of passages at least one careful reading before answering the questions. Try to distinguish main ideas from supporting ideas, and opinions or attitudes from factual, objective information. Note transitions from one idea to the next and identify the relationships among the different ideas or parts of a passage, or between the two passages in Comparative Reading sets. Consider how and why an author makes points and draws conclusions. Be sensitive to implications of what the passages say.

You may find it helpful to mark key parts of passages. For example, you might underline main ideas or important arguments, and you might circle transitional words—"although," "nevertheless," "correspondingly," and the like—that will help you map the structure of a passage. Also, you might note descriptive words that will help you identify an author's attitude toward a particular idea or person.

Answering the Questions

- Always read all the answer choices before selecting the best answer. The best answer choice is the one that most accurately and completely answers the question being posed.

- Respond to the specific question being asked. Do not pick an answer choice simply because it is a true statement. For example, picking a true statement might yield an incorrect answer to a question in which you are asked to identify an author's position on an issue, since you are not being asked to evaluate the truth of the author's position but only to correctly identify what that position is.

- Answer the questions only on the basis of the information provided in the selection. Your own views, interpretations, or opinions, and those you have heard from others, may sometimes conflict with those expressed in a reading selection; however, you are expected to work within the context provided by the reading selection. You should not expect to agree with everything you encounter in Reading Comprehension passages.

THE WRITING SAMPLE

On the day of the test, you will be asked to write one sample essay. LSAC does not score the writing sample, but copies are sent to all law schools to which you apply. According to a 2006 LSAC survey of 157 United States and Canadian law schools, almost all use the writing sample in evaluating at least some applications for admission. Failure to respond to writing sample prompts and frivolous responses have been used by law schools as grounds for rejection of applications for admission.

In developing and implementing the writing sample portion of the LSAT, LSAC has operated on the following premises: First, law schools and the legal profession value highly the ability to communicate effectively in writing. Second, it is important to encourage potential law students to develop effective writing skills. Third, a sample of an applicant's writing, produced under controlled conditions, is a potentially useful indication of that person's writing ability. Fourth, the writing sample can serve as an independent check on other writing submitted by applicants as part of the admission process. Finally, writing samples may be useful for diagnostic purposes related to improving a candidate's writing.

The writing prompt presents a decision problem. You are asked to make a choice between two positions or courses of action. Both of the choices are defensible, and you are given criteria and facts on which to base your decision. There is no "right" or "wrong" position to take on the topic, so the quality of each test taker's response is a function not of which choice is made, but of how well or poorly the choice is supported and how well or poorly the other choice is criticized.

The LSAT writing prompt was designed and validated by legal education professionals. Since it involves writing based on fact sets and criteria, the writing sample gives applicants the opportunity to demonstrate the type of argumentative writing that is required in law school, although the topics are usually nonlegal.

You will have 35 minutes in which to plan and write an essay on the topic you receive. Read the topic and the accompanying directions carefully. You will probably find it best to spend a few minutes considering the topic and organizing your thoughts before you begin writing. In your essay, be sure to develop your ideas fully, leaving time, if possible, to review what you have written. Do not write on a topic other than the one specified. Writing on a topic of your own choice is not acceptable.

No special knowledge is required or expected for this writing exercise. Law schools are interested in the reasoning, clarity, organization, language usage, and writing mechanics displayed in your essay. How well you write is more important than how much you write. Confine your essay to the blocked, lined area on the front and back of the separate Writing Sample Response Sheet. Only that area will be reproduced for law schools. Be sure that your writing is legible.

TAKING THE PREPTEST UNDER SIMULATED LSAT CONDITIONS

One important way to prepare for the LSAT is to simulate the day of the test by taking a practice test under actual time constraints. Taking a practice test under timed conditions helps you to estimate the amount of time you can afford to spend on each question in a section and to determine the question types on which you may need additional practice.

Since the LSAT is a timed test, it is important to use your allotted time wisely. During the test, you may work only on the section designated by the test supervisor. You cannot devote extra time to a difficult section and make up that time on a section you find easier. In pacing yourself, and checking your answers, you should think of each section of the test as a separate minitest.

Be sure that you answer every question on the test. When you do not know the correct answer to a question, first eliminate the responses that you know are incorrect, then make your best guess among the remaining choices. Do not be afraid to guess as there is no penalty for incorrect answers.

When you take a practice test, abide by all the requirements specified in the directions and keep strictly within the specified time limits. Work without a rest period. When you take an actual test, you will have only a short break—usually 10–15 minutes—after SECTION III.

When taken under conditions as much like actual testing conditions as possible, a practice test provides very useful preparation for taking the LSAT.

Official directions for the four multiple-choice sections and the writing sample are included in this PrepTest so that you can approximate actual testing conditions as you practice.

To take the test:

- Set a timer for 35 minutes. Answer all the questions in SECTION I of this PrepTest. Stop working on that section when the 35 minutes have elapsed.

- Repeat, allowing yourself 35 minutes each for sections II, III, and IV.

- Set the timer again for 35 minutes, then prepare your response to the writing sample topic at the end of this PrepTest.

- Refer to "Computing Your Score" for the PrepTest for instruction on evaluating your performance. An answer key is provided for that purpose.

The practice test that follows consists of four sections corresponding to the four scored sections of the June 2014 LSAT. Also reprinted is the June 2014 unscored writing sample topic.

General Directions for the LSAT Answer Sheet

The actual testing time for this portion of the test will be 2 hours 55 minutes. There are five sections, each with a time limit of 35 minutes. The supervisor will tell you when to begin and end each section. If you finish a section before time is called, you may check your work on that section **only;** do not turn to any other section of the test book and do not work on any other section either in the test book or on the answer sheet.

There are several different types of questions on the test, and each question type has its own directions. **Be sure you understand the directions for each question type before attempting to answer any questions in that section.**

Not everyone will finish all the questions in the time allowed. Do not hurry, but work steadily and as quickly as you can without sacrificing accuracy. You are advised to use your time effectively. If a question seems too difficult, go on to the next one and return to the difficult question after completing the section. **MARK THE BEST ANSWER YOU CAN FOR EVERY QUESTION. NO DEDUCTIONS WILL BE MADE FOR WRONG ANSWERS. YOUR SCORE WILL BE BASED ONLY ON THE NUMBER OF QUESTIONS YOU ANSWER CORRECTLY.**

ALL YOUR ANSWERS MUST BE MARKED ON THE ANSWER SHEET. Answer spaces for each question are lettered to correspond with the letters of the potential answers to each question in the test book. After you have decided which of the answers is correct, blacken the corresponding space on the answer sheet. **BE SURE THAT EACH MARK IS BLACK AND COMPLETELY FILLS THE ANSWER SPACE.** Give only one answer to each question. If you change an answer, be sure that all previous marks are **erased completely.** Since the answer sheet is machine scored, incomplete erasures may be interpreted as intended answers. **ANSWERS RECORDED IN THE TEST BOOK WILL NOT BE SCORED.**

There may be more question numbers on this answer sheet than there are questions in a section. Do not be concerned, but be certain that the section and number of the question you are answering matches the answer sheet section and question number. Additional answer spaces in any answer sheet section should be left blank. Begin your next section in the number one answer space for that section.

LSAC takes various steps to ensure that answer sheets are returned from test centers in a timely manner for processing. In the unlikely event that an answer sheet is not received, LSAC will permit the examinee either to retest at no additional fee or to receive a refund of his or her LSAT fee. **THESE REMEDIES ARE THE ONLY REMEDIES AVAILABLE IN THE UNLIKELY EVENT THAT AN ANSWER SHEET IS NOT RECEIVED BY LSAC.**

Score Cancellation

Complete this section only if you are absolutely certain you want to cancel your score. **A CANCELLATION REQUEST CANNOT BE RESCINDED. IF YOU ARE AT ALL UNCERTAIN, YOU SHOULD NOT COMPLETE THIS SECTION.**

To cancel your score from this administration, you **must:**

A. fill in both ovals here ...... ○ ○

AND

B. read the following statement. Then sign your name and enter the date. **YOUR SIGNATURE ALONE IS NOT SUFFICIENT FOR SCORE CANCELLATION. BOTH OVALS ABOVE MUST BE FILLED IN FOR SCANNING EQUIPMENT TO RECOGNIZE YOUR REQUEST FOR SCORE CANCELLATION.**

I certify that I wish to cancel my test score from this administration. I understand that my request is irreversible and that my score will not be sent to me or to the law schools to which I apply.

_____

Sign your name in full

_____

Date

FOR LSAC USE ONLY ●

HOW DID YOU PREPARE FOR THE LSAT?
(Select all that apply.)

Responses to this item are voluntary and will be used for statistical research purposes only.

○ By studying the free sample questions available on LSAC's website.
○ By taking the free sample LSAT available on LSAC's website.
○ By working through official LSAT *PrepTests*, *ItemWise*, and/or other LSAC test prep products.
○ By using LSAT prep books or software **not** published by LSAC.
○ By attending a commercial test preparation or coaching course.
○ By attending a test preparation or coaching course offered through an undergraduate institution.
○ Self study.
○ Other preparation.
○ No preparation.

CERTIFYING STATEMENT

Please write the following statement. Sign and date.

I certify that I am the examinee whose name appears on this answer sheet and that I am here to take the LSAT for the sole purpose of being considered for admission to law school. I further certify that I will neither assist nor receive assistance from any other candidate, and I agree not to copy, retain, or transmit examination questions in any form or discuss them with any other person.

_____

_____

_____

_____

_____

_____

_____

_____

SIGNATURE: _____   TODAY'S DATE: ___/___/___
                                              MONTH DAY YEAR

A

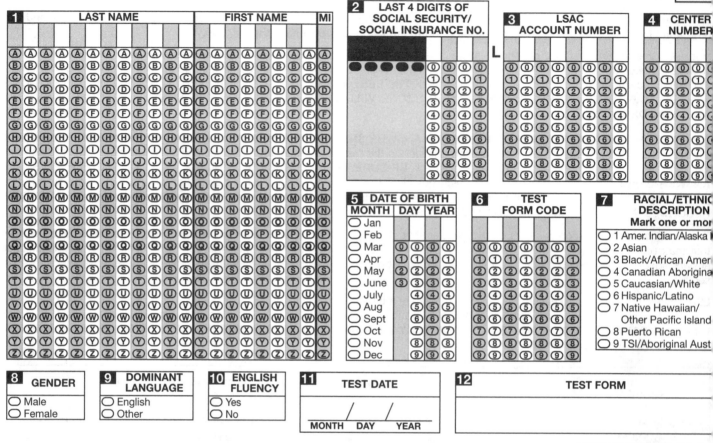

1 LAST NAME | **FIRST NAME** | **MI**

2 LAST 4 DIGITS OF SOCIAL SECURITY/ SOCIAL INSURANCE NO.

3 LSAC ACCOUNT NUMBER

4 CENTER NUMBER

5 DATE OF BIRTH

MONTH	DAY	YEAR
Jan		
Feb		
Mar		
Apr		
May		
June		
July		
Aug		
Sept		
Oct		
Nov		
Dec		

6 TEST FORM CODE

7 RACIAL/ETHNIC DESCRIPTION
Mark one or mor[e]
- 1 Amer. Indian/Alaska
- 2 Asian
- 3 Black/African Amer
- 4 Canadian Aboriginal
- 5 Caucasian/White
- 6 Hispanic/Latino
- 7 Native Hawaiian/ Other Pacific Island
- 8 Puerto Rican
- 9 TSI/Aboriginal Aust

8 GENDER
- Male
- Female

9 DOMINANT LANGUAGE
- English
- Other

10 ENGLISH FLUENCY
- Yes
- No

11 TEST DATE
MONTH / DAY / YEAR

12 TEST FORM

Law School Admission Test

Mark one and only one answer to each question. Be sure to fill in completely the space for your intended answer choice. If you erase, do so completely. Make no stray marks.

13 TEST BOOK SERIAL NO.

14 PLEASE PRINT INFORMATION

LAST NAME

FIRST NAME

DATE OF BIRTH

SECTION 1	SECTION 2	SECTION 3	SECTION 4	SECTION 5
1 A B C D E	1 A B C D E	1 A B C D E	1 A B C D E	1 A B C D E
2 A B C D E	2 A B C D E	2 A B C D E	2 A B C D E	2 A B C D E
3 A B C D E	3 A B C D E	3 A B C D E	3 A B C D E	3 A B C D E
4 A B C D E	4 A B C D E	4 A B C D E	4 A B C D E	4 A B C D E
5 A B C D E	5 A B C D E	5 A B C D E	5 A B C D E	5 A B C D E
6 A B C D E	6 A B C D E	6 A B C D E	6 A B C D E	6 A B C D E
7 A B C D E	7 A B C D E	7 A B C D E	7 A B C D E	7 A B C D E
8 A B C D E	8 A B C D E	8 A B C D E	8 A B C D E	8 A B C D E
9 A B C D E	9 A B C D E	9 A B C D E	9 A B C D E	9 A B C D E
10 A B C D E	10 A B C D E	10 A B C D E	10 A B C D E	10 A B C D E
11 A B C D E	11 A B C D E	11 A B C D E	11 A B C D E	11 A B C D E
12 A B C D E	12 A B C D E	12 A B C D E	12 A B C D E	12 A B C D E
13 A B C D E	13 A B C D E	13 A B C D E	13 A B C D E	13 A B C D E
14 A B C D E	14 A B C D E	14 A B C D E	14 A B C D E	14 A B C D E
15 A B C D E	15 A B C D E	15 A B C D E	15 A B C D E	15 A B C D E
16 A B C D E	16 A B C D E	16 A B C D E	16 A B C D E	16 A B C D E
17 A B C D E	17 A B C D E	17 A B C D E	17 A B C D E	17 A B C D E
18 A B C D E	18 A B C D E	18 A B C D E	18 A B C D E	18 A B C D E
19 A B C D E	19 A B C D E	19 A B C D E	19 A B C D E	19 A B C D E
20 A B C D E	20 A B C D E	20 A B C D E	20 A B C D E	20 A B C D E
21 A B C D E	21 A B C D E	21 A B C D E	21 A B C D E	21 A B C D E
22 A B C D E	22 A B C D E	22 A B C D E	22 A B C D E	22 A B C D E
23 A B C D E	23 A B C D E	23 A B C D E	23 A B C D E	23 A B C D E
24 A B C D E	24 A B C D E	24 A B C D E	24 A B C D E	24 A B C D E
25 A B C D E	25 A B C D E	25 A B C D E	25 A B C D E	25 A B C D E
26 A B C D E	26 A B C D E	26 A B C D E	26 A B C D E	26 A B C D E
27 A B C D E	27 A B C D E	27 A B C D E	27 A B C D E	27 A B C D E
28 A B C D E	28 A B C D E	28 A B C D E	28 A B C D E	28 A B C D E
29 A B C D E	29 A B C D E	29 A B C D E	29 A B C D E	29 A B C D E
30 A B C D E	30 A B C D E	30 A B C D E	30 A B C D E	30 A B C D E

THE PREPTEST

SECTION I

Time—35 minutes

27 Questions

Directions: Each set of questions in this section is based on a single passage or a pair of passages. The questions are to be answered on the basis of what is stated or implied in the passage or pair of passages. For some of the questions, more than one of the choices could conceivably answer the question. However, you are to choose the best answer; that is, the response that most accurately and completely answers the question, and blacken the corresponding space on your answer sheet.

In the last half-century, firefighters in North America have developed a powerful system for fighting wildfires using modern technology. But at the same time, foresters and ecologists are increasingly
(5) aware that too much firefighting can be worse than none at all. Over the millennia, many forest ecosystems have evolved in such a way that they are dependent on periodic fires for renewal and for limiting damage when fires do occur. Ancient ponderosa forests, for
(10) example, were stable in part because low-intensity fires maintained open forests with low levels of fuel for future fires. These fires burned lightly around the bases of mature trees, leaving these trees alive and clearing the understory of brush and young trees.
(15) Scientists can easily count the regular recurrence of fires in these forests over the centuries by examining the scars left on trunks; the typical interval between fires could be as short as 5 years and rarely extended beyond 25 years.
(20) If fires are kept out of forests, however, deadwood and other fuels build up; then, when fire is sparked by lightning or some other cause, what results is a fire so large that it leaves total devastation. Such fires often kill off wildlife that might escape low-intensity fires,
(25) and they also reach the crowns of centuries-old trees, destroying them and ultimately enabling rains to erode the unprotected topsoil. Because of the relative success of fire-suppression efforts, many forests, including ponderosa forests, have now been free of fire for
(30) 50 years or longer, leaving them vulnerable to these devastating crown fires. It is therefore increasingly necessary for land managers in North America to strive to manage rather than eliminate fires; land management policies should recognize the essential
(35) role that fire plays in many ecosystems.
Fire behavior depends on the complex interaction of three factors—topography, weather, and fuel—and since topography is fixed and weather is unpredictable, fuel is the only element that land managers can
(40) control. Land managers should therefore focus their efforts on fuel. A new kind of wildfire management that is designed to simulate the natural role of fire through a combination of selective harvesting and prescribed fires is the most promising method for
(45) controlling fuel. Selective timber harvesting focuses on smaller trees—markets for this smaller material do exist—leaving the larger, fire-tolerant trees on the land and thinning the forest, thereby re-creating the conditions that allow for low-intensity burns.
(50) Prescribed fire management includes both the intentional lighting of controlled burns and the policy

of allowing fires set by lightning to burn when the weather is damp enough to reduce the risk of extensive damage. Once fuels are reduced by these fires,
(55) maintenance burns at 15- to 20-year intervals will be needed. When wildfires inevitably occur, they will be more easily controlled and do much less damage.

1. The primary purpose of the passage is to

(A) claim that ideological dogma may be impeding the enactment of a fundamental and necessary policy change

(B) compare the actual effects that have resulted from two different policies designed to have the same effect

(C) contend that a recently implemented policy requires a substantial increase in funding

(D) recommend a fundamental policy change in light of evidence that current policy has created undesirable conditions

(E) argue that two seemingly contradictory goals of a policy are actually compatible in a fundamental way

2. By "maintenance burns" (line 55) the author most clearly refers to

(A) the low-intensity fires that regularly occurred in ancient forests

(B) fires that reduce the population density of mature trees

(C) the types of fires that are likely to occur in North American forest ecosystems today

(D) a type of fire that used to occur at intervals greater than 50 years

(E) naturally or intentionally set fires that are allowed to burn to eliminate fuel

GO ON TO THE NEXT PAGE.

3. Which one of the following ~~logically complete the last pa~~

(A)   However, if homes we~~i~~
proximity to forests, th~~e~~
property would be limite~~d~~

(B)   Unfortunately, until foreste~~rs~~
dangers posed by excess fu~~el~~
proposals are likely to meet ~~resistance from~~
the forestry community.

(C)   But even with these policies, w~~hich may take~~
some years to achieve their inte~~nded effect,~~
large, devastating fires will rema~~in a threat in~~
the near term.

(D)   Yet, because smaller trees will likely ~~not produce a~~
profit for timber companies, the eco~~logical~~
benefits of the new plans must be wei~~ghed~~
carefully against their economic impact.

(E)   But given the large financial resources nee~~ded~~
to operate a prescribed fire management
system, the chances of such policies being
implemented are quite small.

4. The author cites the factors of topography, weather, and fuel in the last paragraph primarily as part of

(A)   the support provided for the contention that land managers must focus on fuel to reduce the risk of crown fires

(B)   an argument that, given the interaction among these factors, land managers' efforts to control wildfires will always be somewhat ineffective

(C)   an attempt to provide a clearer understanding of why forest fires have become unnaturally devastating

(D)   an argument that specific fuel types and forest densities are dependent on topographic and weather conditions

(E)   the suggestion that fires started by lightning will continue to be a factor in wildfire suppression efforts

5. The passage provides the most support for inferring that which one of the following is true of ancient ponderosa forests?

(A)   Ponderosas that thrived in these forests probably differed genetically from modern ponderosas in subtle, though significant, ways.

(B)   The population density of trees in these forests was generally lower than it is in many ponderosa forests today.

(C)   Weather patterns in these forests were substantially different from weather patterns in ponderosa forests today.

(D)   The diversity of plant species was greater in these forests than it is in ponderosa forests today.

~~(E)~~   In addition to clearing out excess fuel, periodic low-intensity fires helped to control wildlife populations in these forests.

~~It~~ can be inferred from the passage that the author would be most likely to regard a policy in which all forest fires that were started by lightning were allowed to burn until they died out naturally as

(A)   a viable means of restoring forests currently vulnerable to catastrophic fires to a cycle of periodic low-intensity fires

(B)   an essential component of a new wildfire management plan that would also involve the regulation of timber harvests

(C)   beneficial to forests that have centuries-old trees, though harmful to younger forests

(D)   currently too extreme and likely to cause the destruction land managers are seeking to avoid

(E)   politically infeasible given the public perception of the consequences of such fires

GO ON TO THE NEXT PAGE.

The government of Mali passed a law against excavating and exporting the wonderful terra-cotta sculptures from the old city of Djenne-jeno, but it could not enforce it. And it certainly could not afford
(5) to fund thousands of archaeological excavations. The result was that many fine Djenne-jeno terra-cotta sculptures were illicitly excavated in the 1980s and sold to foreign collectors who rightly admired them. Because these sites were looted, much of what we
(10) would most like to know about this culture—much that we could have learned had the sites been preserved by careful archaeology—may now never be known.

It has been natural to condemn such pillaging. And, through a number of declarations from UNESCO
(15) and other international bodies, a protective doctrine has evolved concerning the ownership of many forms of cultural property (the "UNESCO doctrine"). Essentially the doctrine provides that cultural artifacts should be regarded as the property of the culture. For
(20) an individual belonging to that culture, such works are, using UNESCO's terminology, part of an "artistic and cultural patrimony." Further, a number of countries have strengthened the UNESCO doctrine by declaring all antiquities that originate within their borders to be
(25) state property that cannot be freely exported.

Accordingly, it seems reasonable that the government of Mali, within whose borders the Djenne-jeno antiquities are buried, be the one to regulate excavating Djenne-jeno and to decide where
(30) the statues should go. Regrettably, and this is a painful irony, regulations prohibiting export and requiring repatriation can discourage recording and preserving information about cultural antiquities, one of the key reasons for the UNESCO regulations. For example, if
(35) someone in London sells a figure from Djenne-jeno with documentation that it came out of the ground there after the regulations were implemented, then the authorities committed to the restitution of objects taken illegally out of Mali have the very evidence
(40) they need to seize the figure.

Suppose that from the beginning, Mali had been helped by UNESCO to exercise its trusteeship of the Djenne-jeno terra-cotta sculptures by licensing excavations and educating people to recognize that
(45) such artifacts have greater value when they are removed carefully from the earth with accurate records of location. Suppose Mali had required that objects be recorded and registered before leaving the excavation site, and had imposed a tax on exported objects to
(50) fund acquisitions of important pieces for the national museum. The excavations encouraged by such a system may have been less well conducted and less informative than proper, professionally administered excavations by accredited archaeologists. Some people
(55) would still have avoided the rules. But would this not have been better than what actually happened?

7. Which one of the following most accurately expresses the main point of the passage?

(A) Declarations from UNESCO and other international bodies concerning the ownership of cultural artifacts gave rise to a doctrine based on the notion of artistic and cultural patrimony.

(B) Preserving cultural knowledge at sites like Djenne-jeno requires solutions that are more flexible than simply passing laws prohibiting the excavation and export of antiquities.

(C) Rather than acceding to the dictates of international bodies, countries like Mali must find their own unique solutions to problems concerning the preservation of cultural heritage.

(D) The government of Mali should have exercised its trusteeship of the Djenne-jeno terra-cotta sculptures by licensing only accredited archaeologists for the excavations.

(E) The idea that a culture's artistic and cultural patrimony is the property of the state does more harm than good in countries like Mali.

8. The passage indicates that some countries have made use of the UNESCO doctrine in which one of the following ways?

(A) requiring the origins of all antiquities sold to collectors to be fully documented

(B) restricting the export of antiquities and declaring all antiquities originating within the country's borders to be state property

(C) adopting plans to teach people to recognize that antiquities have greater value when they are removed carefully from the earth with accurate records of location

(D) encouraging trade in a particular ancient culture's artifacts among countries each of which contains within its boundaries a portion of that ancient culture's territory

(E) committing substantial resources to the restoration of antiquities taken illegally out of countries like Mali

9. The author asks the reader to suppose that Mali had imposed a tax on exported objects (lines 49–51) primarily in order to

(A) draw attention to the role of museums in preserving cultural patrimonies

(B) praise one of the Malian government's past policies concerning cultural antiquities

(C) present one part of a more pragmatic approach to regulating the trade in cultural antiquities

(D) suggest a means of giving people who excavate cultural antiquities incentive to keep careful records

(E) highlight a flaw in the UNESCO doctrine

10. The author of the passage would be most likely to agree with which one of the following statements about UNESCO?

(A)   It can play an important role in stemming abuses that arise from the international trade in cultural artifacts.
(B)   Its stance on cultural artifacts emerged for the most part in response to Mali's loss of terra-cotta sculptures from Djenne-jeno.
(C)   It is more effective with initiatives that involve individual states than initiatives that involve several states.
(D)   It pays too little attention to the concerns of countries like Mali.
(E)   Its effectiveness in limiting the loss of cultural knowledge has been hampered by inadequate funding.

11. The author of the passage would be most likely to agree with which one of the following statements about regulations governing the trade in cultural antiquities in countries like Mali?

(A)   Such regulations must be approved by archaeologists before being enacted.
(B)   Such regulations must have as their goal maximizing the number of cultural antiquities that ultimately remain in these countries.
(C)   Such regulations can be beneficial even if not all people strictly comply with them.
(D)   Such regulations must be accompanied by very strict punishments for violators.
(E)   Such regulations are most effective when they are very simple and easily understood.

12. The author of the passage would be most likely to agree with which one of the following statements about cultural antiquities?

(A)   They must be owned and protected by a country's national museum.
(B)   They must remain within the boundaries of the country in which they were found.
(C)   They are too valuable to be owned exclusively by the state.
(D)   They should be excavated by professional archaeologists when possible.
(E)   They belong to whoever finds them and registers them with the state.

13. Which one of the following is an element of the author's attitude toward foreign collectors of terra-cotta sculptures from Djenne-jeno?

(A)   appreciation of their efforts to preserve cultural artifacts
(B)   approval of their aesthetic judgment
(C)   dismay at their failure to take action against illegal exportation of cultural artifacts
(D)   frustration with their lack of concern for the people of Mali
(E)   sympathy with their motives

GO ON TO THE NEXT PAGE.

The following passage is based on an article published in 1987.

Medical practitioners are ethically required to prescribe the best available treatments. In ordinary patient-physician interactions, this obligation is unproblematic, but when physicians are clinical
(5) researchers in comparative studies of medical treatments, special issues arise. Comparative clinical trials involve withholding one or more of the treatments from at least one group of patients. Traditionally, most physicians and ethicists have agreed that in testing a
(10) new treatment on a patient population for which there exists a currently accepted treatment, the participating physicians should have no opinion as to which treatment is clinically superior—a state of mind usually termed "equipoise."
(15) Unfortunately, the conception of equipoise that is typically employed—which I will term "theoretical equipoise"—may be too strict. Theoretical equipoise exists only when the overall evidence for each of two treatment regimens is judged by each clinical
(20) researcher to be exactly balanced—an ideal hardly attainable in practice. Clinical researchers commonly have some preference for one of the treatments being tested, an intuitive preference perhaps, or one based on their interpretation and balancing of various sources
(25) of evidence. Even if researchers judged the evidence to be balanced at the start of a comparative clinical trial, such a balance would be extremely fragile, liable to be "tipped" by small accretions of evidence as the study progresses. Consequently, if the standard of
(30) theoretical equipoise is adhered to, few comparative clinical trials could commence and even fewer could proceed to completion.

These difficulties associated with theoretical equipoise suggest that a different notion of equipoise
(35) should be developed, one that I will label "clinical equipoise." Clinical equipoise would impose rigorous ethical standards on comparative clinical trials without unreasonably constricting them. One reason for conducting comparative clinical trials is to resolve a
(40) current or imminent conflict in the expert clinical community over what treatment is to be preferred for patients with a given illness. It could be that the standard treatment is A but new evidence suggests that B will be superior. Medical experts may be
(45) divided as to which treatment is better, with each side recognizing that opposing experts can differ honestly in their interpretation of the evidence.

The very absence of consensus within the expert clinical community is what makes clinical equipoise
(50) possible. One or more of a comparative clinical trial's researchers may have a decided treatment preference based on their assessments of the evidence. But that is no ethical bar to participation in the trial. The clinical researchers must simply each recognize that their less-
(55) favored treatment is preferred by a sizable constituency within the medical profession as a whole.

14. The author's primary purpose in the passage is to

(A) explain the difference between two conceptions of an ethical standard together with how these conceptions would affect comparative clinical trials

(B) argue for a more reasonable, less restrictive interpretation of an ethical requirement than the one traditionally given by ethicists and physicians

(C) demonstrate that a change in the standards governing comparative clinical trials will endanger the ability of researchers to derive valuable information from such trials

(D) demonstrate the need for clinical researchers to more closely examine the conceptions embodied in the ethical standards to which these researchers adhere

(E) argue for a change in the scientific methods used for gathering evidence in comparative clinical trials

15. The primary purpose of the second paragraph of the passage is to

(A) provide a view that contrasts with arguments in favor of clinical equipoise

(B) explore the factors underlying physicians' preferences regarding competing treatments

(C) undermine the moral principle that underlies the theory of theoretical equipoise

(D) state the main difficulty with adhering to the standards of theoretical equipoise

(E) illustrate the conflicts inherent in the general notion of equipoise

16. According to the passage, which one of the following is true?

(A) Comparative clinical trials that meet the standard of theoretical equipoise generally present no ethical problems.

(B) Clinical researchers are often forced to suspend comparative clinical trials prematurely because initial data from the trials strongly favors one treatment over another.

(C) A clinical trial comparing treatments is not rendered unethical merely because one of the participating physicians has come to favor one of the treatments over the other.

(D) A comparative clinical trial that meets the standard of clinical equipoise would therefore also meet the standard of theoretical equipoise.

(E) Medical researchers generally try to conduct comparative clinical trials in accordance with the standard of clinical equipoise.

GO ON TO THE NEXT PAGE.

17. Suppose two medical treatments are being compared in a clinical trial for their effectiveness in treating a condition. Based on the passage, which one of the following scenarios would be significantly more likely to jeopardize theoretical equipoise than clinical equipoise?

(A) The initial results of the trial so strikingly favored one treatment that they were published and widely disseminated before the study was even half over; as a result, most physicians who specialize in treating the condition came to favor the more effective treatment before the trial had ended.

(B) Preliminary results in the trial suggest that the two treatments are equally effective in treating the condition; but these results are not reported while the trial is underway and thus few in the expert clinical community are aware of them.

(C) Several of the physicians participating in the trial think that one treatment is more effective at treating the condition than the other; in this they agree with the consensus view within the expert clinical community.

(D) Initial results from the trial convince several of the participating physicians that one treatment more effectively treats the condition than the other does; this does not affect their recognition of the lack of consensus among experts in treating the disease.

(E) There is consensus among physicians participating in the trial that both treatments are equally effective at treating the condition; however, there is no consensus within the expert medical community as to the relative effectiveness of the treatments.

18. Which one of the following most accurately expresses the main point of the passage?

(A) The ethical requirement that physicians prescribe the best available treatment to their patients is jeopardized by an overly strict conception of equipoise.

(B) Medical research conducted through comparative clinical trials is able to achieve more if the ethical requirements it is bound by are not overly restrictive.

(C) It is sometimes ethically acceptable for a physician to participate in a clinical trial in which the physician has a decided treatment preference in favor of one of the treatments being tested.

(D) Clinical equipoise should be adopted because it is less likely to unreasonably constrict the conducting of comparative clinical trials than is theoretical equipoise.

(E) Even though comparative clinical trials often fail to meet the standard of theoretical equipoise, they should not, for that reason, be considered unethical.

19. As used in line 41 of the passage, the term "community" most nearly refers to a group of people

(A) who focus on a common set of problems using a shared body of knowledge

(B) who live and work in the same geographical area as one another

(C) who share opinions that differ significantly from those of other groups

(D) whose association with one another is based on their similar ethical values

(E) whose similar research methods are employed in unrelated disciplines

20. According to the passage, which one of the following is true?

(A) Most clinical trials that are conducted meet the appropriate ethical standards.

(B) Clinical trials would be conducted more often if there were a more reasonable ethical standard in place.

(C) Theoretical equipoise imposes an ethical standard on clinical trials that is rarely if ever met.

(D) Most physicians and ethicists believe that the currently accepted ethical requirements for comparative clinical trials are adequate.

(E) Most comparative clinical trials are undertaken to help resolve a conflict of opinion in the expert clinical community concerning the best available treatment.

21. The author's argument in the third and fourth paragraphs would be most weakened if which one of the following were true?

(A) In most comparative clinical trials, the main purpose is to prove definitively that a treatment considered best by a consensus of relevant experts is in fact superior to the alternative being tested.

(B) Physicians participating in comparative clinical trials rarely ask to leave the trials because early data favors one of the treatments being tested over another.

(C) The number of comparative clinical trials that are conducted annually is increasing rapidly, but the level of ethical oversight of these trials is decreasing.

(D) Medical ethicists are more inclined than are clinical researchers to favor an ethical requirement based on theoretical equipoise over one based on clinical equipoise.

(E) In clinical trials comparing two treatments, it rarely occurs that researchers who begin the trial with no preference for either of the treatments later develop a strong preference on the basis of data obtained early in the study.

GO ON TO THE NEXT PAGE.

Passage A

In 1994, Estonia became the first country to introduce a "flat tax" on personal and corporate income. Income is taxed at a single uniform rate of 26 percent: no schedule of rates, no deductions. So far eight
(5) countries have followed Estonia's example. An old idea that for decades elicited the response, "Fine in theory, just not practical in the real world," seems to be working as well in practice as it does on the blackboard.

Practical types who said that flat taxes cannot
(10) work offer a further instant objection, once they are shown such taxes working, namely, that they are unfair. Enlightened countries, it is argued, have "progressive" tax systems, requiring high-income earners to forfeit a bigger share of their incomes in tax than low-income
(15) earners have to pay. A flat tax seems to rule this out in principle.

Not so. A flat tax on personal incomes combines a threshold (that is, an exempt amount) with a single rate of tax on all income above it. The extent to which
(20) such a system is progressive can be varied within wide limits using just these two variables. Under the systems operating in most developed countries, the incentives for high-income earners to avoid tax (legally or otherwise) are enormous; and the opportunities to do
(25) so, which arise from the very complexity of the codes, are commensurately large. So it is unsurprising that high-income earners usually pay about as much tax under new flat-tax regimes as they would have paid under the previous codes.

Passage B

(30) A lot of people don't understand graduated, as opposed to "flat," taxes. They think that if you make more money you pay a higher rate on your entire earnings, which seems unfair. Actually, graduated progressive taxes treat all taxpayers equally.
(35) Every taxpayer pays the same rate on equivalent layers of income. People in higher brackets don't pay the higher rate on their entire income, only on the portion of income over a specified amount. People, not dollars, are treated equally.

(40) All people are created equal, but not all dollars are created equal. Earnings of the working poor go almost entirely for survival expenses such as food, shelter, and clothing. At that level, every dollar is critical; even a small difference causes tremendous
(45) changes in quality of life. Middle-income earners are still very conscious of expenses, but have much greater flexibility in absorbing small fluctuations in income.

Even some of the flat tax proposals recognize this, and want to exempt a primary layer from the tax
(50) system. So, since they recognize that survival dollars are different from discretionary dollars, why go suddenly from one extreme (paying no taxes) to the other (paying the top rate)? Since flat tax proposals are supposed to bring in the same total amount of tax
(55) revenue, if the working poor are going to pay less and the high-income earners are going to pay less, it is naturally going to fall on the middle class to make up the difference.

22. Both passages are concerned with answering which one of the following questions?

(A) Can a flat tax be implemented?
(B) Do graduated progressive taxes treat all taxpayers equally?
(C) Can a flat tax be fair to all taxpayers?
(D) What are some objections to progressive taxes?
(E) Do flat tax regimes reduce illegal tax avoidance?

23. Both passages seek to advance their arguments by means of which one of the following?

(A) accusing opponents of shifting their ground
(B) citing specific historical developments as evidence
(C) arguing on the basis of an analogy
(D) employing rhetorical questions
(E) correcting alleged misunderstandings

24. Which one of the following, if true of countries that have gone from a graduated progressive tax system to a flat tax, would most support the position of passage B over that of passage A?

(A) Revenues from taxation have remained the same as before.
(B) The tax codes in these countries have been greatly simplified.
(C) Most high-income taxpayers believe that they remain overtaxed.
(D) Middle-income taxpayers tend to pay higher taxes than before.
(E) Some legislators favor a return to a graduated progressive system.

25. Which one of the following is a conclusion for which passage A argues but that passage B does not address?

(A) that exempting a threshold amount enables a flat tax to avoid unfairness
(B) that flat tax proposals are not practical in the real world
(C) that higher taxes on high-income earners inhibit investment and economic growth
(D) that a flat tax decreases opportunities and incentives for high-income earners to avoid tax
(E) that a progressive tax is unfair to taxpayers who end up paying more

GO ON TO THE NEXT PAGE.

26. The authors of the two passages would be most likely to disagree over whether

(A) a flat tax system can be progressive
(B) high-income earners would pay less under a flat tax system than under a graduated progressive system
(C) flat tax systems are fine in theory but cannot be put into practice
(D) graduated progressive systems make higher-income taxpayers pay a higher rate on their entire earnings
(E) all of an individual's income should be subject to taxation

27. Which one of the following, if true, would be the most reasonable response for the author of passage B to make to the final argument of passage A?

(A) Even under a flat-tax regime, it will be possible for some with high incomes to avoid taxes by underreporting their incomes.
(B) Existing tax codes allow tax avoidance by those with high incomes mainly because they contain loopholes and special deductions, not because they are graduated.
(C) It is unfair to those with high incomes to single them out as tax avoiders, since people at all income levels have been known to try to avoid taxes, sometimes illegally.
(D) Most taxpayers prefer a system that affords them opportunities for avoiding taxes over one that does not afford such opportunities.
(E) The goal of reducing tax avoidance would be advanced by eliminating income taxes altogether in favor of taxes on consumption of goods and services.

S T O P

IF YOU FINISH BEFORE TIME IS CALLED, YOU MAY CHECK YOUR WORK ON THIS SECTION ONLY.
DO NOT WORK ON ANY OTHER SECTION IN THE TEST.

SECTION II

Time—35 minutes

26 Questions

Directions: The questions in this section are based on the reasoning contained in brief statements or passages. For some questions, more than one of the choices could conceivably answer the question. However, you are to choose the best answer; that is, the response that most accurately and completely answers the question. You should not make assumptions that are by commonsense standards implausible, superfluous, or incompatible with the passage. After you have chosen the best answer, blacken the corresponding space on your answer sheet.

1. Treat training consists of rewarding dogs with edible treats whenever they respond appropriately to commands. Most dogs will quickly learn what they need to do to receive a treat, so this appears to be an effective training method. However, most dogs who have been treat-trained will not obey commands unless they are shown a treat. Since you cannot always have treats on hand, you should instead use praise and verbal correction to train your dog.

Which one of the following principles, if valid, most helps to justify the reasoning above?

(A) The more quickly a dog learns to respond to a stimulus, the more likely it is that the owner will continue to use that stimulus.

(B) The more often a dog is given a stimulus, the more likely it is that the dog will obey its owner's command even when the owner does not provide that stimulus.

(C) A dog should be trained by the method that results in a high obedience rate in at least some circumstances.

(D) A dog should be trained to respond to a stimulus that its owner can supply in all situations.

(E) A dog should not be trained by a method that has not proven to be effective for any other dogs.

2. Archaeologist: For 2,000 years the ancient Sumerians depended on irrigation to sustain the agriculture that fed their civilization. But eventually irrigation built up in the soil toxic levels of the salts and other impurities left behind when water evaporates. When its soil became unable to support agriculture, Sumerian civilization collapsed. A similar fate is thus likely to befall modern civilizations that continue to rely heavily on irrigation for agriculture.

Which one of the following, if true, most weakens the archaeologist's argument?

(A) Most modern civilizations could not feed themselves through agriculture without relying heavily on irrigation.

(B) Factors unrelated to the use of irrigation would probably have caused Sumerian civilization to collapse sooner or later.

(C) Many modern farmers use irrigation techniques that avoid the buildup of salts and other toxic impurities in the soil.

(D) Many modern civilizations do not rely to any significant extent on irrigation for agriculture.

(E) The soil of ancient Sumeria already contained some toxic salts and other impurities before the Sumerians started using irrigation for agriculture.

3. Researcher: Dinosaur fossils come in various forms, including mineralized bones and tracks in dried mud flats. However, mineralized dinosaur bones and dinosaur tracks in dried mud flats are rarely found together. This isn't surprising, because creatures that scavenged dinosaur carcasses most likely frequented mud flats to find food.

Which one of the following, if true, would most strengthen the researcher's argument?

(A) Dinosaur tracks are also found in locations other than mud flats.

(B) Scavengers commonly drag a carcass away from the site where it was found.

(C) Researchers have found more fossil dinosaur tracks than fossil dinosaur bones.

(D) Dinosaur fossils other than mineralized bone or tracks in dried mud flats are quite common.

(E) It takes longer for bone to mineralize than it takes for tracks to dry in mud flats.

GO ON TO THE NEXT PAGE.

4. Electric stovetop burners would cause fewer fires if their highest temperature were limited to 350ºC (662ºF), which provides more than enough heat for efficient and effective cooking. The lowest temperature at which cooking oil and most common fibers ignite is 387ºC, and electric burners on high go well above 700ºC.

Which one of the following most accurately expresses the conclusion drawn in the argument?

(A) Electric stovetop burners would cause fewer fires if their highest temperature were limited to 350ºC.

(B) A maximum temperature of 350ºC provides more than enough heat for efficient and effective cooking.

(C) The lowest ignition temperature for cooking oil and most common fibers is 387ºC.

(D) Electric burners on high go well above 700ºC.

(E) Electric stovetop burners cause fires because they go well above 700ºC when set on high.

5. Jenkins maintains that the movie *Firepower* was not intended to provoke antisocial behavior, arguing that, on the contrary, it is in the interest of *Firepower*'s director to prevent such behavior. Yet Jenkins's conclusion must be rejected, because the movie has clearly produced antisocial behavior among many of those who have seen it.

The reasoning in the argument is flawed in that it

(A) rejects an argument on the grounds that it was offered by a person who was biased

(B) concludes from a mere correlation between certain phenomena that those phenomena are causally related

(C) infers that something is true of a whole solely on the grounds that it is true of a part of the whole

(D) overlooks the possibility that people can act in a way that is contrary to their expressed interest

(E) concludes from the mere fact that an action had a certain effect that the effect was intended by the person who performed the action

6. The word "loophole" is a loaded, partisan word, one that implies wrongdoing and scandal. When "loophole" creeps into news stories, they start to read like editorials. So news reporters should not use the term "loophole" in their stories unless they provide evidence of wrongdoing.

Which one of the following principles, if valid, most helps to justify the reasoning in the argument?

(A) Making use of a loophole never constitutes wrongdoing or scandal.

(B) Editorials should meet the same journalistic standards as news stories.

(C) News stories need to give evidence to back up any suggestions of misconduct.

(D) Editorial writers should be free to use loaded, partisan words.

(E) News reporters should not report on wrongdoing and scandal that is not a matter of public interest.

7. Expert: Some people claim that, since food production has thus far increased faster than population has, there is no need to be concerned about widespread food shortages. These people fail to recognize that the planet's resources allow for food to be produced at only a few times the current amount, beyond which no increase in production will be possible. Thus, widespread food shortages are inevitable.

Which one of the following, if true, most strengthens the expert's reasoning?

(A) The world's food resources, though limited, are renewable.

(B) Food resources from the world's oceans will eventually be fully utilized.

(C) The world's population has recently remained fairly stable because of falling birth rates.

(D) Periodic regional food shortages have occurred at least briefly throughout history.

(E) Population will continue to grow at least briefly when food production has reached its maximum level.

GO ON TO THE NEXT PAGE.

8. In the earliest video games, the player typically controlled the movements of a simple icon on the screen. But in newer video games, players often control the movements of detailed human figures—a feature possible because of the greater technical sophistication of these games. It is hard for players to identify with these figures, since the players can see that the figures represent other people. Thus, in this respect the technical sophistication of the newer video games often makes them less compelling to players.

The conclusion of the argument can be properly drawn if which one of the following is assumed?

(A) There are no newer, more technically sophisticated video games in which the player controls the movements of a simple icon on the screen.

(B) Most early video games in which the player controlled a simple icon on the screen were in other respects less compelling to players than newer video games.

(C) The technical sophistication necessary for creating detailed human figures in video games cannot in itself make those video games fully compelling even to players who identify with those figures.

(D) When players cannot easily identify with the figure or icon whose movements they control in a video game, they usually find that game less compelling than it otherwise would be.

(E) If some aspect of a video game's technical sophistication makes it less compelling to players, then that video game contains a human figure with whom it is difficult for players to identify.

9. There are many agricultural regions in North America where the growing season is long enough to allow pumpkin production well into autumn with no risk of frost. Nonetheless, pumpkin production in North America is concentrated in regions with long, cold winters, where the growing season is delayed and pumpkin crops are exposed to risk of damage or destruction by early autumn frosts.

Which one of the following, if true, most helps to resolve the apparent discrepancy in the information above?

(A) Pumpkins are usually grown to reach maturity in autumn.

(B) Pumpkins depend on bees for pollination, and bees are active only in warm weather.

(C) More pumpkins are sold to consumers in regions of North America with long growing seasons than to those in regions with short growing seasons.

(D) Prolonged cold temperatures kill soil-borne fungus and other sources of disease that would kill or seriously damage pumpkins.

(E) Most of the pumpkin seed used by growers in North America is produced in areas where the growing season is long, and plants used for seed production are protected in greenhouses.

10. Council chair: The traditional code of parliamentary procedure contains a large number of obscure, unnecessary rules, which cause us to quibble interminably over procedural details and so to appear unworthy of public confidence. Admittedly, the code is entrenched and widely accepted. But success in our endeavors depends on the public's having confidence in our effectiveness. Therefore, it is imperative that we adopt the alternate code, which has been in successful use elsewhere for several years.

Which one of the following, if true, most seriously undermines the chair's conclusion?

(A) The council's use of the problematic rules in the traditional code is intermittent.

(B) Those who have adopted the alternate code sometimes attempt to use it to obscure their opponents' understanding of procedures.

(C) Revision of the traditional code is underway that will eliminate the problematic rules.

(D) It is not always reasonable to adopt a different code in order to maintain the public's confidence.

(E) The alternate code contains few provisions that have thus far been criticized as obscure or unnecessary.

GO ON TO THE NEXT PAGE.

11. Businesses frequently use customer surveys in an attempt to improve sales and increase profits. However, a recent study of the effectiveness of these surveys found that among a group of businesses that sold similar products, profits declined in most of the businesses that used surveys during the course of the study but not in most of the businesses that did not use any surveys during the course of the study.

Which one of the following, if true, most helps to explain why the profits of businesses that did not use customer surveys did not decline while the profits of those that used surveys did decline?

(A) When one business increases its profits, its competitors often report a decline in profits.

(B) Some businesses routinely use customer surveys.

(C) Most businesses of the kind included in the study generally administer customer surveys only as a response to complaints by customers.

(D) Customers who complete surveys do not always respond accurately to all the questions on the survey.

(E) Some of the businesses included in the study did not analyze the results of the customer surveys they conducted.

12. Humans' emotional tendencies are essentially unchanged from those of the earliest members of our species. Accordingly, although technology makes possible a wider range of individual and societal choices than in centuries past, humans are generally unable to choose more wisely.

The argument depends on assuming which one of the following?

(A) Humans have undergone no significant changes since the origin of the species.

(B) Humans who make wise choices are generally in control of their emotions.

(C) Human history cannot make humans any wiser unless humans are emotionally disposed to heed the lessons of history.

(D) Regardless of the range of choices available to humans, they choose on the basis of their emotions alone.

(E) Humans would now be able to make wiser choices than in centuries past only if an essential change had taken place in humans' emotional dispositions.

13. Some ornithologists believe that many species of songbirds are threatened by deforestation. Yet they also claim that, despite recent reforestation, matters continue to worsen, since it is fragmentation of forest rather than reduction of forest size that endangers songbird species. The introduction of open spaces and corridors in forests reduces the distance of songbird nests from unforested areas and thus reduces the songbirds' natural shield from predators.

The claim that there has recently been reforestation plays which one of the following roles in the ornithologists' argument?

(A) It is used as evidence that various species of songbirds will continue to be threatened with extinction.

(B) It is presented as a claim that is rejected by ornithologists who present declining songbird populations as evidence of deforestation.

(C) It is presented as a phenomenon that is compatible with the ornithologists' claim that the threat to songbirds continues to worsen.

(D) It is used as evidence that songbirds' predators will continue to have a habitat and so will continue to pose a threat to songbirds.

(E) It is presented as evidence for the claim that songbirds' predators are threatened by extinction unless they have open spaces and corridors that give them access to their prey.

14. Researchers recently studied the relationship between diet and mood, using a diverse sample of 1,000 adults. It was found that those who ate the most chocolate were the most likely to feel depressed. Therefore, by reducing excessive chocolate consumption, adults can almost certainly improve their mood.

The argument is most vulnerable to criticism on which one of the following grounds?

(A) It improperly infers from the fact that a substance causally contributes to a condition that a reduction in the consumption of the substance is likely to eliminate that condition.

(B) It draws a conclusion about the population as a whole on the basis of a sample that is unlikely to be representative of that population.

(C) It draws a conclusion about a causal relationship between two phenomena from evidence that merely suggests that there is a correlation between those phenomena.

(D) It confuses a condition that is necessary for establishing the truth of the conclusion with a condition that is sufficient for establishing the truth of the conclusion.

(E) Its conclusion is worded too vaguely to evaluate the degree to which the premises support the truth of the conclusion.

GO ON TO THE NEXT PAGE.

15. Among the many temptations of the digital age, manipulation of photographs has proved particularly troublesome for science. Recently, a journal of cellular biology began using a software tool to examine the digital images submitted along with articles for publication. It discovered that dozens of authors had submitted digital images that had been manipulated in ways that violated the journal's guidelines. Clearly, scientific fraud is a widespread problem among the authors submitting to that journal.

Which one of the following is an assumption required by the argument?

(A) The scientists who submitted manipulated images were aware that the journal used software to examine digital images for evidence of manipulation.

(B) The journal requires that all articles submitted for publication include digital images.

(C) Scientific fraud is possible in the field of cellular biology only if the research is documented with digital images.

(D) Many of the scientists who submitted articles with manipulated images did so in order to misrepresent the information conveyed by those images.

(E) Scientific fraud is a widespread problem only among scientists who submit articles to journals of cellular biology.

16. There are already more great artworks in the world than any human being could appreciate in a lifetime, works capable of satisfying virtually any taste imaginable. Thus, contemporary artists, all of whom believe that their works enable many people to feel more aesthetically fulfilled than they otherwise could, are mistaken.

The argument is most vulnerable to criticism on the grounds that it

(A) overlooks the possibility that not all contemporary artists believe that their works enable many people to feel more aesthetically fulfilled than they otherwise could

(B) presumes, without providing justification, that most human beings are inclined to take the time to appreciate many great artworks

(C) presumes, without providing justification, that the value of an artwork depends on the degree to which human beings appreciate it

(D) overlooks the possibility that the work of at least one contemporary artist is appreciated by many people whose access to the great majority of other artworks is severely restricted

(E) presumes, without providing justification, that the number and variety of great artworks already in the world affects the amount of aesthetic fulfillment derivable from any contemporary artwork

17. The government health service has said that it definitely will not pay for patients to take the influenza medicine Antinfia until the drug's manufacturer, PharmCo, provides detailed information about Antinfia's cost-effectiveness. PharmCo has responded that obtaining such information would require massive clinical trials. These trials cannot be performed until the drug is in widespread circulation, something that will happen only if the government health service pays for Antinfia.

If the statements of both the government health service and PharmCo are true, which one of the following is most likely to also be true?

(A) The government health service never pays for any medicine unless that medicine has been shown to be cost-effective.

(B) Antinfia will never be in widespread circulation.

(C) If the government health service does not pay for Antinfia, then many patients will pay for Antinfia themselves.

(D) The government health service should pay for patients to take Antinfia.

(E) Antinfia is not cost-effective.

18. Journalist: Scientists took blood samples from two large, diverse groups of volunteers. All the volunteers in one group reported that they enjoyed eating vegetables, whereas all those in the other group disliked vegetables. When the blood samples from the group that disliked vegetables were analyzed, it was discovered that all the volunteers in that group had a gene in common, the XRV2G gene. This strongly suggests that a dislike of vegetables is, at least in some cases, genetically determined.

The journalist's argument is most vulnerable to criticism on which one of the following grounds?

(A) It presumes that all human traits are genetically determined.

(B) It overlooks the possibility that the volunteers in one or both of the two groups may not have been representative of the human population as a whole in one or more respects.

(C) It overlooks the possibility that even when one phenomenon always produces another phenomenon, the latter phenomenon may often be present when the former is absent.

(D) It overlooks the possibility that even if a dislike of vegetables is genetically determined, it may be strongly influenced by genes other than the XRV2G gene.

(E) It takes for granted that the volunteers in the group that enjoyed eating vegetables did not also all have the XRV2G gene in common.

GO ON TO THE NEXT PAGE.

19. Ana: On libertarian principles, I oppose the proposed smoking ban. It is not the government's business to prevent people from doing things that harm only themselves.

Pankaj: But keep in mind that the ban would apply only to smoking in public places. People could still smoke all they want in private.

The dialogue provides the most support for the claim that Ana and Pankaj disagree over whether

(A)   it is the government's business to prevent people from harming themselves

(B)   government should be restrained by libertarian principles

(C)   the proposed smoking ban is intended to prevent harm only to smokers themselves

(D)   the proposed ban would prohibit smoking in public places

(E)   there are cases in which government should attempt to regulate private behavior

20. Agricultural scientist: Wild apples are considerably smaller than cultivated apples found in supermarkets. In one particular region, archaeologists have looked for remains of cultivated apples dating from 5,000 years ago, around the time people first started cultivating fruit. But the only remains of apples that archaeologists have found from this period are from fruits the same size as the wild apples native to the region. So apples were probably not cultivated in this region 5,000 years ago.

The agricultural scientist's argument is most vulnerable to criticism on the grounds that the argument

(A)   fails to consider that even if a plant was not cultivated in a given region at a specific time, it may have been cultivated in nearby regions at that time

(B)   fails to consider that plants that have been cultivated for only a short time may tend to resemble their wild counterparts much more closely than plants that have been cultivated for a long time

(C)   takes for granted that all apples are either the size of wild apples or the size of the cultivated apples now found in supermarkets

(D)   employs a premise that is incompatible with the conclusion it is supposed to justify

(E)   uses a claim that presupposes the truth of its main conclusion as part of the justification for that conclusion

21. Genuine happiness consists not in pleasurable feelings but instead in one's sense of approval of one's character and projects. Thus the happy life, in fact, tends to be the good life, where the good life is understood not—as it usually is these days—as a life of material well-being but rather as a morally virtuous life.

Which one of the following is an assumption required by the argument?

(A)   A morally virtuous life requires the rejection of material well-being.

(B)   People who approve of their own character and projects tend to lead morally virtuous lives.

(C)   Approval of one's own character and projects tends not to result in pleasurable feelings.

(D)   Attaining happiness is the real goal of people who strive for material well-being.

(E)   Material well-being does not increase one's sense of approval of one's character and projects.

GO ON TO THE NEXT PAGE.

22. The return of organic wastes to the soil is a good solution to waste disposal problems only if the wastes are nontoxic and not too much energy is expended in transporting them. In small-scale organic farming, the wastes are nontoxic and not too much energy is expended in transporting them. Hence, returning organic wastes to the soil is a good way for small-scale organic farms to solve their waste disposal problems.

Which one of the following exhibits flawed reasoning most similar to the flawed reasoning exhibited by the argument above?

(A) Plants thrive if they get an abundance of moisture, light, and nutrients. In greenhouses, plants get an optimal combination of all three, which is why commercially produced plants are so healthy when you first buy them.

(B) When every country has equal access to markets, which will be the case 20 years from now, globalization of markets will provide a way for each country to optimize its use of resources. So, globalization of markets will show the desired results 20 years from now.

(C) To be viable, a business idea must be clear, cost-effective, practical, and responsive to a market demand. Your idea for a website information service has all these properties, so it is viable.

(D) Those competitors—and only those—who meet all of the following criteria are eligible for the award: they must be under 19 years of age, be in secondary school, and have played the sport for at least the two years immediately preceding the competition. You meet all the criteria, so you are eligible.

(E) A meal is nutritious only if it includes both carbohydrates and protein. Almost 80 percent of the calories in what I ate for lunch were from fat, so what I ate for lunch was not nutritious.

23. Scientist: Some colonies of bacteria produce antibiotic molecules called phenazines, which they use to fend off other bacteria. We hypothesize that phenazines also serve as molecular pipelines that give interior bacteria access to essential nutrients in the environment surrounding the colony.

Which one of the following, if true, provides the most support for the scientist's hypothesis?

(A) Bacteria colonies that do not produce phenazines form wrinkled surfaces, thus increasing the number of bacteria that are in direct contact with the surrounding environment.

(B) The rate at which a bacteria colony produces phenazines is determined by the number of foreign bacteria in the environment immediately surrounding the colony.

(C) When bacteria colonies that do not produce phenazines are buried in nutrient-rich soil, they grow as quickly as colonies that do produce phenazines.

(D) Bacteria colonies that produce phenazines are better able to fend off other bacteria than are bacteria colonies that do not produce phenazines.

(E) Within bacteria colonies that produce phenazines, interior bacteria are more likely to die than are bacteria along the edges.

24. Library preservationist: Due to the continual physical deterioration of the medieval manuscripts in our library's collection, we have decided to restore most of our medieval manuscripts that are of widely acknowledged cultural significance, though this means that some medieval manuscripts whose authenticity is suspect will be restored. However, only manuscripts whose safety can be ensured during the restoration process will be restored, and manuscripts that are not frequently consulted by researchers will not be restored.

If all of the library preservationist's statements are true, which one of the following must be true of the medieval manuscripts in the library's collection?

(A) Some of the medieval manuscripts whose authenticity is suspect are frequently consulted by researchers.

(B) All of the medieval manuscripts widely acknowledged to be of cultural significance are manuscripts whose safety can be ensured during the restoration process.

(C) All of the medieval manuscripts whose safety can be ensured during the restoration process are frequently consulted by researchers.

(D) The medieval manuscripts most susceptible to deterioration are those most frequently consulted by researchers.

(E) None of the medieval manuscripts that are rarely consulted by researchers is widely acknowledged to be of cultural significance.

GO ON TO THE NEXT PAGE.

25. Direct-mail advertising usually consists of advertisements for products to be purchased from the home, so the perception that it is bad for the environment is misguided. Because of direct-mail advertising, millions of people buy products by phone or online—products whose purchase would otherwise require the use of a car, thus adding pollutants to the air.

Which one of the following, if true, would most strengthen the argument?

(A) Although the primary intent of most direct-mail advertisers is to convince people to buy products from their homes, direct mail can also lead to increased sales in stores by customers who prefer to see a product prior to purchasing it.

(B) Most of the products purchased in response to direct-mail advertisements would be purchased even without the direct-mail advertisements.

(C) A person who receives and reads a direct-mail advertisement is more likely to purchase the product advertised than is a person who reads an advertisement for a product in a magazine that they subscribe to.

(D) Usually, a company that sends out direct-mail advertisements has good reason to think that the person to whom the advertisement is sent would be more interested in the product than would the average person.

(E) Products purchased as the result of direct-mail advertising comprise an increasingly large portion of the consumer products purchased each year.

26. The older a country is, the more likely it is to be ruled by a monarch. Thus, since most countries are not ruled by monarchs, if a country is particularly new it is probably not ruled by a monarch.

The pattern of reasoning in the argument above is most similar to that in which one of the following arguments?

(A) Most novels are not made into movies. However, the more popular a novel is, the more likely it is to be made into a movie. Thus, if a movie is quite unpopular, it was probably not based on a novel.

(B) Most novels are not made into movies. However, the more popular a movie is, the more likely it is that the movie was based on a novel. Thus, if a novel is particularly popular, it will probably be made into a movie.

(C) Most novels are not made into movies. Moreover, if a novel is particularly unpopular, it will probably not be made into a movie. Thus, the more popular a novel is, the more likely it is to be made into a movie.

(D) Most novels are not made into movies. However, the more popular a novel is, the more likely it is to be made into a movie. Thus, if a novel is quite unpopular, it will probably not be made into a movie.

(E) Most novels are not made into movies. Moreover, the more complex a novel's plot, the less likely the novel is to be made into a movie. Thus, if a novel has a particularly simple plot, it will probably be made into a movie.

S T O P

IF YOU FINISH BEFORE TIME IS CALLED, YOU MAY CHECK YOUR WORK ON THIS SECTION ONLY.
DO NOT WORK ON ANY OTHER SECTION IN THE TEST.

SECTION III
Time—35 minutes
25 Questions

Directions: The questions in this section are based on the reasoning contained in brief statements or passages. For some questions, more than one of the choices could conceivably answer the question. However, you are to choose the best answer; that is, the response that most accurately and completely answers the question. You should not make assumptions that are by commonsense standards implausible, superfluous, or incompatible with the passage. After you have chosen the best answer, blacken the corresponding space on your answer sheet.

1. Dentist: I recommend brushing one's teeth after every meal to remove sugars that facilitate the growth of certain bacteria; these bacteria produce acid that dissolves minerals in tooth enamel, resulting in cavities. And when brushing is not practical, I recommend chewing gum—even gum that contains sugar—to prevent the formation of cavities.

   Which one of the following, if true, would most help to reconcile the dentist's apparently paradoxical recommendations?

   (A) A piece of chewing gum that contains sugar contains far less sugar than does the average meal.
   (B) Tooth decay can be stopped and reversed if it is caught before a cavity develops.
   (C) Chewing gum stimulates the production of saliva, which reduces acidity in the mouth and helps remineralize tooth enamel.
   (D) Sugars can be on teeth for as long as 24 hours before the teeth-damaging bacteria whose growth they facilitate begin to proliferate.
   (E) Chewing gum exercises and relaxes the jaw muscles and so contributes to the overall health of the oral tract.

2. When the ancient fossils of a primitive land mammal were unearthed in New Zealand, they provided the first concrete evidence that the island country had once had indigenous land mammals. Until that discovery, New Zealand had no known native land mammals. The discovery thus falsifies the theory that New Zealand's rich and varied native bird population owes its existence to the lack of competition from mammals.

   Which one of the following, if true, most seriously weakens the argument?

   (A) The unearthed land mammal is only one of several ancient land mammals that were indigenous to New Zealand.
   (B) The recently discovered land mammal became extinct long before the native bird population was established.
   (C) The site at which the primitive land mammal was unearthed also contains the fossils of primitive reptile and insect species.
   (D) Countries with rich and varied native land mammal populations do not have rich and varied native bird populations.
   (E) Some other island countries that are believed to have no native land mammals in fact had indigenous land mammals at one time.

GO ON TO THE NEXT PAGE.

3. Restaurant owner: The newspaper reporter who panned my restaurant acknowledges having no special expertise about food and its preparation. His previous job was as a political reporter. He is a good writer, but he is not a true restaurant critic. A newspaper would never call someone a drama critic who had no special training in theater.

Which one of the following most accurately expresses the conclusion drawn in the restaurant owner's argument?

(A) The newspaper reporter who panned the restaurant acknowledges having no special expertise about food and its preparation.

(B) The previous job of the newspaper reporter who panned the restaurant was as a political reporter.

(C) The newspaper reporter who panned the restaurant is a good writer.

(D) The newspaper reporter who panned the restaurant is not a true restaurant critic.

(E) A newspaper would never call someone a drama critic who had no special training in theater.

4. It has been hypothesized that our solar system was formed from a cloud of gas and dust produced by a supernova—an especially powerful explosion of a star. Supernovas produce the isotope iron-60, so if this hypothesis were correct, then iron-60 would have been present in the early history of the solar system. But researchers have found no iron-60 in meteorites that formed early in the solar system's history, thereby disproving the hypothesis.

Which one of the following is an assumption required by the argument?

(A) If a meteorite is formed early in the solar system's history, it contains chemical elements that are unlikely to be found in gas and dust produced by a supernova.

(B) Other solar systems are not formed from clouds of gas and dust produced by supernovas.

(C) Supernovas do not produce significant quantities of any form of iron other than iron-60.

(D) Researchers have found iron-60 in meteorites that were formed relatively late in the solar system's history.

(E) If there had been iron-60 present in the early history of the solar system, it would be found in meteorites formed early in the solar system's history.

5. Safety expert: Tuna is often treated with carbon monoxide so that it will not turn brown as it ages. Treating tuna with carbon monoxide does not make it harmful in any way. Nonetheless, there is a danger that such treatment will result in more people getting sick from eating tuna.

Which one of the following, if true, most helps to resolve the apparent discrepancy in the safety expert's statements?

(A) Workers in fish processing plants can be sickened by exposure to carbon monoxide if the appropriate safety procedures are not followed at those plants.

(B) Over the last several years, tuna consumption has increased in most parts of the world.

(C) Tuna that is treated with carbon monoxide provides no visible indication when it has spoiled to the point that it can cause food poisoning.

(D) Treating tuna with carbon monoxide is the only way to keep it from turning brown as it ages.

(E) Most consumers strongly prefer tuna that is not brown because they believe that brown tuna is not fresh.

6. Astrophysicist: Gamma ray bursts (GRBs)—explosions of powerful radiation from deep space—have traditionally been classified as either "short" or "long," terms that reflect the explosion's relative duration. However, an unusual GRB has been sighted. Its duration was long, but in every other respect it had the properties of a short GRB. Clearly, the descriptive labels "short" and "long" have now outlived their usefulness.

The conclusion of the astrophysicist's argument is most strongly supported if which one of the following is assumed?

(A) No other GRBs with unusual properties have been sighted.

(B) The classification of GRBs can sometimes be made on the basis of duration alone.

(C) Properties other than duration are more important than duration in the proper classification of the unusual GRB.

(D) GRBs cannot be classified according to the different types of cosmic events that create them.

(E) Descriptive labels are easily replaced with nondescriptive labels such as "type I" and "type II."

GO ON TO THE NEXT PAGE.

7. In one study, hospital patients' immune systems grew stronger when the patients viewed comic videos. This indicates that laughter can aid recovery from illness. But much greater gains in immune system strength occurred in the patients whose tendency to laugh was greater to begin with. So hospital patients with a greater tendency to laugh are helped more in their recovery from illness even when they laugh a little than other patients are helped when they laugh a greater amount.

The argument is most vulnerable to criticism on the grounds that it

(A) overlooks the possibility that the patients whose tendency to laugh was greater to begin with laughed more at the comic videos than did the other patients

(B) fails to address adequately the possibility that the patients whose tendency to laugh was greatest to begin with already had stronger immune systems than the other patients

(C) presumes, without providing justification, that hospital patients have immune systems representative of those of the entire population

(D) takes for granted that the gains in immune system strength did not themselves influence the patients' tendency to laugh

(E) presumes, without providing justification, that the patients whose tendency to laugh was greatest to begin with recovered from their illnesses more rapidly than the other patients

8. A study of guppy fish shows that a male guppy will alter its courting patterns in response to feedback from a female guppy. Males with more orange on one side than the other were free to vary which side they showed to a female. Females were drawn to those males with more orange showing, and males tended to show the females their more orange side when courting.

Which one of the following, if true, provides the most support for the argument?

(A) When a model of a female guppy was substituted for the female guppy, male guppies still courted, but were not more likely to show their side with more orange.

(B) In many other species females show a preference for symmetry of coloring rather than quantity of coloring.

(C) No studies have been done on whether male guppies with more orange coloring father more offspring than those with less orange coloring.

(D) Female guppies have little if any orange coloring on their sides.

(E) The male and female guppies were kept in separate tanks so they could see each other but not otherwise directly interact.

9. Politician: Some proponents of unilateral nuclear arms reduction argue that it would encourage other countries to reduce their own nuclear arsenals, eventually leading to an international agreement on nuclear arms reduction. Our acting on the basis of this argument would be dangerous, because the argument ignores the countries presently on the verge of civil wars. These countries, many of which have nuclear capability, cannot be relied upon to conform to any international military policy.

Which one of the following most accurately expresses the conclusion of the politician's argument?

(A) Countries that are on the verge of civil wars are unlikely to agree to reduce either their nuclear arms or their conventional weapons.

(B) Unilateral nuclear arms reduction by the politician's country would encourage all countries to reduce their nuclear arsenals.

(C) Many countries cannot be relied upon to disclose the extent of their nuclear capability.

(D) It is unlikely that an international agreement on nuclear disarmament will ever be achieved.

(E) It is risky for the politician's country to unilaterally reduce nuclear arms in hopes of achieving an international agreement on arms reduction.

GO ON TO THE NEXT PAGE.

10. Advertisement: Auto accidents are the most common cause of whiplash injury, a kind of injury that is caused by a sudden sharp motion of the neck. However, many other types of accidents can produce a sudden sharp motion of the neck and thereby result in whiplash injury. A sudden sharp motion of the neck can be caused by a fall, a bump on the head, or even by being shoved from behind. That is why you should insist on receiving Lakeside Injury Clinic's complete course of treatment for whiplash after any accident that involves a fall or a bump on the head.

Which one of the following, if true, provides the strongest basis for criticizing the reasoning in the advertisement?

(A) Being shoved from behind rarely causes whiplash.
(B) Auto accidents often involve falling or being bumped on the head.
(C) Nonautomobile accidents other than those involving falls or bumps on the head also occasionally cause whiplash injuries.
(D) It is very uncommon for falling or being bumped on the head to result in a sudden sharp motion of the neck.
(E) The appropriate treatment for whiplash caused by a fall or a bump on the head is no different from that for whiplash caused by an auto accident.

11. A group of citizens opposes developing a nearby abandoned railroad grade into a hiking trail. Its members argue that trail users will likely litter the area with food wrappers and other debris. But this objection is groundless. Most trail users will be dedicated hikers who have great concern for the environment. Consequently, development of the trail should proceed.

The argument above is flawed in that it

(A) bases its conclusion mainly on a claim that an opposing argument is weak
(B) illicitly infers that because each member of a set has a certain property that set itself has the property
(C) illicitly assumes as one of its premises the contention it purports to show
(D) illicitly infers that an attribute of a few users of the proposed trail will characterize a majority of users of the trail
(E) attacks the citizens in the group rather than their objection to developing the trail

12. For years, university administrators, corporations, and government agencies have been predicting an imminent and catastrophic shortage of scientists and engineers. But since there is little noticeable upward pressure on the salaries of scientists and engineers, and unemployment is as high in these fields as any other, these doomsayers are turning out to be wrong.

Which one of the following would, if true, most strengthen the argument above?

(A) The proportion of all research in science and engineering being carried out by corporations is larger than it was five years ago.
(B) Most students choose fields of study that offer some prospect of financial success.
(C) The number of students in university programs in science and engineering has increased significantly in the last five years.
(D) Certain specializations in science and engineering have an oversupply of labor and others have shortages.
(E) The knowledge and skills acquired during university programs in science and engineering need to be kept current through periodic retraining and professional experience.

13. Rhonda: As long as the cost is not too great, you should use your time, energy, or money to help others. People who are active participants in charitable causes have richer lives than miserly hermits, however prosperous the hermits may be.

Brad: You should ignore the problems of complete strangers and focus your generosity on your immediate relatives and close friends, since these are the people who will remember your sacrifices and return the kindness when you yourself need help.

Which one of the following principles, if valid, would most help to justify both Rhonda's and Brad's arguments?

(A) One should always do what will produce the most benefit for the most people.
(B) One should treat others as one expects to be treated by them.
(C) One should act in ways that will benefit oneself.
(D) One should make sacrifices for others only if they will eventually return the favor.
(E) One should always act in a manner that one can reflect on with pride.

GO ON TO THE NEXT PAGE.

14. Columnist: Wildlife activists have proposed that the practice of stringing cable TV lines from the same poles that carry electric power lines should be banned because cable TV lines, while electrically neutral themselves, make it easier for animals to climb near electric power lines, risking electrocution. This particular argument for banning the practice fails, however, since some animals are electrocuted by power lines even where cable TV lines are all underground.

Which one of the following most accurately describes a flaw in the columnist's reasoning?

(A) It takes a sufficient condition for an argument's being inadequate to be a necessary condition for its being inadequate.

(B) It rejects an argument for a proposal merely on the grounds that the proposal would not completely eliminate the problem it is intended to address.

(C) It fails to consider the additional advantageous effects that a proposal to address a problem might have.

(D) It rejects an argument by criticizing the argument's proponents rather than by criticizing its substance.

(E) It rejects a proposal to address a problem merely on the grounds that other proposals to address the problem would also be effective.

15. The ancient reptile *Thrinaxodon*, an ancestor of mammals, had skull features suggesting that it had sensory whiskers. If *Thrinaxodon* had whiskers, it clearly also had hair on other parts of its body, which would have served as insulation that regulated body temperature. Therefore, *Thrinaxodon* was probably warm-blooded, for such insulation would be of little use to a cold-blooded animal.

Which one of the following most accurately describes the role played in the argument by the statement that if *Thrinaxodon* had whiskers, it clearly also had hair on other parts of its body, which would have served as insulation that regulated body temperature?

(A) It is a premise offered in support of the conclusion that insulation regulating body temperature would be of little use to a cold-blooded animal.

(B) It is a premise offered in support of the main conclusion drawn in the argument.

(C) It is a conclusion for which the claim that *Thrinaxodon* had skull features suggesting that it had sensory whiskers is offered as support.

(D) It is a statement of a hypothesis that the argument attempts to show is false.

(E) It is offered as an explanation of the phenomenon described by the argument's main conclusion, but it is not itself used to provide support for that conclusion.

16. Economist: Currently, many countries rely primarily on taxing income to fund government expenditures. But taxing income does nothing to promote savings and investment. Taxing consumption, on the other hand, would encourage savings. The most important challenge facing these countries is improving their economies, and the only way to accomplish this is to increase their savings rates. Hence, _____.

Which one of the following most logically completes the economist's argument?

(A) most governments should stop taxing savings and investment

(B) the economies of countries will rapidly improve if their governments adopt tax policies that encourage savings and investment

(C) in most countries taxes on consumption alone could raise adequate revenues to fund government expenditures

(D) the tax laws of many countries should be revised to focus on taxing consumption rather than income

(E) it is detrimental to the economic improvement of any country to continue to tax income

17. Meade: People who are injured as a result of their risky behaviors not only cause harm to themselves but, because we all have important ties to other people, inevitably impose emotional and financial costs on others. To protect the interests of others, therefore, governments are justified in outlawing behavior that puts one's own health at risk.

Which one of the following principles, if valid, most undermines the reasoning in Meade's argument?

(A) Endangering the social ties that one has to other people is itself a harm to oneself.

(B) People who have important ties to others have a personal obligation not to put their own health at risk.

(C) Governments are not justified in limiting an individual's behavior unless that behavior imposes emotional or financial costs on others.

(D) Preventing harm to others is not by itself a sufficient justification for laws that limit personal freedom.

(E) People's obligation to avoid harming others outweighs their obligation to avoid harming themselves.

GO ON TO THE NEXT PAGE.

18. Sanderson intentionally did not tell his cousin about overhearing someone say that the factory would close, knowing that if he withheld this information, his cousin would assume it would remain open. Clearly this was morally wrong. After all, lying is morally wrong. And making a statement with the intention of misleading someone is lying. True, it was Sanderson's failing to state something that misled his cousin. Yet there is no moral difference between stating and failing to state if they are done with the same intention.

Which one of the following is an assumption required by the argument?

(A) Sanderson believed that his cousin would not want to be informed about the factory closing.

(B) No one ever told Sanderson's cousin about the factory closing.

(C) Sanderson believed that the factory would in fact be closing.

(D) Sanderson would have lied to his cousin if his cousin had asked him whether the factory would be closing.

(E) Sanderson had something to gain by his cousin's continuing to believe that the factory would remain open.

19. After a judge has made the first ruling on a particular point of law, judges must follow that precedent if the original ruling is not contrary to the basic moral values of society. In the absence of precedent, when judges' own legal views do not contradict any widespread public opinion—and only then—they may abide by their own legal views in deciding a case.

Of the rulings described below, which one conforms most closely to the principles stated above?

(A) Judge Swoboda is confronted with a legal issue never before decided. Realizing that his own view on the issue contradicts what most people believe, he nonetheless issues a ruling that accords with his own legal views.

(B) Judge Valenzuela decides, in the absence of any precedent, whether children as young as twelve can be legally tried as adults. There is overwhelming public support for trying children twelve and older as adults, a practice that violates Judge Valenzuela's personal moral views. So Judge Valenzuela rules, in keeping with his own legal beliefs, against trying twelve-year-olds as adults.

(C) Judge Levinsky sets a legal precedent when she rules that the "starfish exception" applies to children. In deciding a later case concerning the starfish exception, Judge Wilson adheres to his own legal views rather than Judge Levinsky's ruling, even though he does not believe that Judge Levinsky's ruling opposes the basic moral values of society.

(D) Judge Watanabe must decide a case that depends on an issue for which no legal precedent exists. There is no widespread public opinion on the issue, so Judge Watanabe rules against the defendant because that conforms to her own legal view about the issue.

(E) Judge Balila rules against the defendant because doing so conforms to her own views about the legal issues involved. However, this ruling is contrary to relevant precedents, all of which conform to the basic moral values of society.

GO ON TO THE NEXT PAGE.

20. Neuroscientists subjected volunteers with amusia—difficulty telling different melodies apart and remembering simple tunes—to shifts in pitch comparable to those that occur when someone plays one piano key and then another. The volunteers were unable to discern a difference between the tones. But the volunteers were able to track timed sequences of musical tones and perceive slight changes in timing.

The statements above, if true, most strongly support which one of the following hypotheses?

(A) People who are unable to discern pitch compensate by developing a heightened perception of timing.

(B) Amusia results more from an inability to discern pitch than from an inability to discern timing.

(C) People who are unable to tell pitches apart in isolation are able to do so in the context of a melody by relying upon timing.

(D) The ability to tell melodies apart depends on the discernment of pitch alone and not at all on the perception of timing.

(E) Whereas perception of timing can apparently be learned, discernment of pitch is most likely innate.

21. Literary critic: There is little of social significance in contemporary novels, for readers cannot enter the internal world of the novelist's mind unless they experience that world from the moral perspective of the novel's characters. But in contemporary novels, the transgressions committed by some characters against others are sensationalistic spectacles whose only purpose is to make readers wonder what will happen next, rather than events whose purpose is to be seen as the injustices they are.

Which one of the following principles, if valid, would most help to justify the literary critic's argument?

(A) An artist who wants to engage the moral sensibilities of his or her audience should not assume that forms of artistic expression that previously served this purpose continue to do so.

(B) A novelist who wants to make a reader empathize with a victim of injustice should avoid sensationalistic spectacles whose only purpose is to make readers wonder what will happen next.

(C) A work of art is socially important only if it engages the moral sensibilities of its audience.

(D) If a novel allows a reader to understand injustice from the point of view of its victims, it will be socially significant.

(E) Novels have social significance only to the extent that they allow readers to enter the internal world of the novelist's mind.

22. A recent study revealed that people who follow precisely all the standard recommendations for avoidance of infection by pathogenic microorganisms in meat-based foods are more likely to contract diseases caused by these pathogens than are those who deviate considerably from the standard recommendations. Hence, the standard recommendations for avoidance of infection by these pathogens must be counterproductive.

The argument is most vulnerable to criticism on the grounds that it fails to take into account which one of the following possibilities?

(A) Pathogenic microorganisms can reproduce in foods that are not meat-based.

(B) Many people do follow precisely all the standard recommendations for avoidance of infection by pathogenic microorganisms in meat-based foods.

(C) Not all diseases caused by microorganisms have readily recognizable symptoms.

(D) Preventing infection by pathogenic microorganisms is simply a matter of following the appropriate set of recommendations.

(E) Those most concerned with avoiding pathogenic infections from meat-based foods are those most susceptible to them.

GO ON TO THE NEXT PAGE.

23. No nonfiction book published by Carriage Books has ever earned a profit. Since Carriage Books earned a profit on every book it published last year, it clearly did not publish a nonfiction book last year.

The pattern of reasoning in the argument above is most similar to that in which one of the following arguments?

(A) No actor represented by the talent agent Mira Roberts has ever won an important role in a major movie. Since every actor represented by Ms. Roberts had at least one important acting role last year, it is clear that none of those actors worked in a movie last year.

(B) No hotel owned by the Bidmore Group specializes in serving business travelers. Since the Cray Springs Hotel is owned by the Bidmore Group, it clearly does not specialize in serving business travelers.

(C) Pranwich Corporation has never given a bonus to an employee in its marketing division. Since Pranwich gave bonuses to every one of its systems analysts last year, it is clear that the company employed no systems analysts in its marketing division at that time.

(D) James Benson has never done business with the city of Waldville. Since Waldville only maintains business files on individuals that it does business with, it clearly does not have a business file on James Benson.

(E) Conway Flooring has never installed hardwood flooring for any customer in Woodridge. Since Conway Flooring has had a lot of customers in Woodridge, the company clearly does not install hardwood flooring.

24. All unemployed artists are sympathetic to social justice. And no employed artists are interested in the prospect of great personal fame.

If the claims made above are true, then which one of the following must be true?

(A) If there are artists interested in the prospect of great personal fame, they are sympathetic to social justice.

(B) All artists uninterested in the prospect of great personal fame are sympathetic to social justice.

(C) Every unemployed artist is interested in the prospect of great personal fame.

(D) If an artist is sympathetic to social justice, that artist is unemployed.

(E) All artists are either sympathetic to social justice or are interested in the prospect of great personal fame.

25. The police department has two suspects for the burglary that occurred last night, Schaeffer and Forster. Schaeffer has an ironclad alibi, so Forster must be the burglar.

Which one of the following arguments exhibits a flawed pattern of reasoning that is most similar to that exhibited by the argument above?

(A) It has been known for some time that the Wrightsburg Zoo might build a new primate house and that it might refurbish its polar bear exhibit. There is now good reason to believe the zoo will build a new primate house. Therefore, the zoo will not refurbish its polar bear exhibit.

(B) If Watson, a robbery suspect, had been picked out of a police lineup by the victim, then charging Watson with robbery would have been reasonable. But the victim did not pick Watson out of the lineup. So Watson should not be charged.

(C) If Iano Industries does not borrow money so that it can upgrade its factories, it will be unable to compete. While it is undesirable for Iano to take on more debt, being unable to compete would be even worse. So Iano should borrow the money needed to upgrade its factories.

(D) Baxim Corporation announced last year that it was considering moving its headquarters to Evansville and that it was also considering moving to Rivertown. But Baxim has now decided not to move to Evansville. Thus, we can be sure that Baxim will move to Rivertown.

(E) The only viable candidates in the mayoral race are Slater and Gonzales. Political analysts believe that Slater has little chance of winning. Therefore, it is likely that Gonzales will win the election.

S T O P

IF YOU FINISH BEFORE TIME IS CALLED, YOU MAY CHECK YOUR WORK ON THIS SECTION ONLY.
DO NOT WORK ON ANY OTHER SECTION IN THE TEST.

SECTION IV

Time—35 minutes

23 Questions

Directions: Each group of questions in this section is based on a set of conditions. In answering some of the questions, it may be useful to draw a rough diagram. Choose the response that most accurately and completely answers each question and blacken the corresponding space on your answer sheet.

Questions 1–6

A radio station airs hourly news updates every morning. Each update consists of exactly five reports—two of general interest: international and national; and three of local interest: sports, traffic, and weather. Each update must be structured as follows:

  There are exactly two segments, the first segment containing three reports and the second segment containing two.

  Within each segment, reports are ordered by length, from longest to shortest.

  Each segment contains at least one report of local interest.

  The national report is always the longest of the five reports.

  The sports report is always the shortest of the five reports.

  The international report is always longer than the weather report.

1. Which one of the following could be an accurate matching of reports to their segments, with the reports listed in order from earliest to latest?

(A)   first segment: international, national, sports
       second segment: traffic, weather
(B)   first segment: national, international, sports
       second segment: weather, traffic
(C)   first segment: national, international, weather
       second segment: sports, traffic
(D)   first segment: national, weather, international
       second segment: traffic, sports
(E)   first segment: traffic, weather, sports
       second segment: national, international

GO ON TO THE NEXT PAGE.

2. If the traffic report is the last report in the first segment, then which one of the following must be true?

(A) The national report is the first report in the first segment.
(B) The international report is the second report in the first segment.
(C) The weather report is the second report in the first segment.
(D) The national report is the first report in the second segment.
(E) The sports report is the last report in the second segment.

3. If the national report is the first report in the second segment, then exactly how many of the reports are there any one of which could be the first report in the first segment?

(A) one
(B) two
(C) three
(D) four
(E) five

4. Which one of the following CANNOT be true?

(A) The international report is the first report in the first segment.
(B) The national report is the first report in the first segment.
(C) The national report is the first report in the second segment.
(D) The weather report is the first report in the first segment.
(E) The weather report is the last report in the second segment.

5. The order of the reports is fully determined if which one of the following is true?

(A) The international report is the last report in the first segment.
(B) The national report is the first report in the first segment.
(C) The national report is the first report in the second segment.
(D) The sports report is the last report in the second segment.
(E) The weather report is the last report in the first segment.

6. If the traffic report is the first report in the first segment, then which one of the following could be true?

(A) The international report is the first report in the second segment.
(B) The national report is the second report in the first segment.
(C) The weather report is the second report in the first segment.
(D) The weather report is the first report in the second segment.
(E) The weather report is the last report in the second segment.

GO ON TO THE NEXT PAGE.

Questions 7–12

On a single day, a realtor will show a client five houses, exactly one house in each of five neighborhoods—Quarry, Riverton, Shelburne, Townsend, and Valencia. Each house will be shown to the client exactly once. The order in which the houses are shown is subject to the following constraints:

The house in Riverton must be shown either first or second.

The house in Townsend must be shown either first or fifth.

The third house shown must be the house in Quarry or the house in Valencia.

The house in Quarry cannot be shown either immediately before or immediately after the house in Shelburne.

7. If the house in Quarry is shown fourth, which one of the following must be true?

(A) The house in Riverton is shown first.
(B) The house in Riverton is shown second.
(C) The house in Shelburne is shown second.
(D) The house in Townsend is shown first.
(E) The house in Valencia is shown third.

GO ON TO THE NEXT PAGE.

8. The order in which the houses are shown is fully determined if which one of the following is true?

(A) The house in Quarry is shown third.
(B) The house in Riverton is shown first.
(C) The house in Shelburne is shown second.
(D) The house in Townsend is shown fifth.
(E) The house in Valencia is shown fourth.

9. If the house in Shelburne is shown earlier than the house in Quarry, which one of the following must be true?

(A) The house in Quarry is shown fourth.
(B) The house in Riverton is shown second.
(C) The house in Shelburne is shown first.
(D) The house in Townsend is shown fifth.
(E) The house in Valencia is shown third.

10. Which one of the following could be true?

(A) The house in Quarry is shown first.
(B) The house in Quarry is shown fifth.
(C) The house in Valencia is shown first.
(D) The house in Valencia is shown second.
(E) The house in Valencia is shown fifth.

11. If the house in Valencia is shown third, which one of the following must be true?

(A) The house in Quarry is shown fourth.
(B) The house in Riverton is shown second.
(C) The house in Shelburne is shown first.
(D) The house in Shelburne is shown fourth.
(E) The house in Townsend is shown fifth.

12. Which one of the following, if substituted for the constraint that the house in Riverton must be shown either first or second, would have the same effect on the order in which the houses are shown?

(A) The house in Riverton cannot be shown fourth.
(B) The house in Riverton must be shown earlier than the house in Valencia.
(C) The house in Valencia must be shown either third or fourth.
(D) The house in Quarry must be shown either immediately before or immediately after the house in Riverton.
(E) If the house in Townsend is not shown fifth, then it must be shown immediately before the house in Riverton.

GO ON TO THE NEXT PAGE.

Questions 13–18

Five artifacts—V, W, X, Y, and Z—recovered from a sunken ship are each known to have originated in Iceland, Norway, or Sweden. These artifacts, together with the surviving fragments of a cargo list, have enabled historians to determine the following:

    W and Y originated in the same country.

    X originated in Norway or Sweden.

    More of the artifacts originated in Iceland than in Norway.

    If V originated in Iceland, then Z originated in Sweden.

13. Which one of the following could be an accurate matching of the artifacts to their origins?

(A)   Iceland: V, W
           Norway: X
           Sweden: Y, Z

(B)   Iceland: W, Y
           Norway: none
           Sweden: V, X, Z

(C)   Iceland: W, Y
           Norway: V, Z
           Sweden: X

(D)   Iceland: V, W, Y
           Norway: Z
           Sweden: X

(E)   Iceland: W, X, Y
           Norway: Z
           Sweden: V

GO ON TO THE NEXT PAGE.

14. If Y and Z originated in Iceland, then what is the minimum number of artifacts that originated in Sweden?

    (A)   zero
    (B)   one
    (C)   two
    (D)   three
    (E)   four

15. Which one of the following CANNOT be true?

    (A)   V and X both originated in Norway.
    (B)   V and Y both originated in Iceland.
    (C)   W and Z both originated in Iceland.
    (D)   W and Z both originated in Sweden.
    (E)   W and Y both originated in Norway.

16. If W and X originated in Sweden, then which one of the following must be true?

    (A)   None of the artifacts originated in Norway.
    (B)   None of the artifacts originated in Iceland.
    (C)   V originated in Sweden.
    (D)   Z originated in Iceland.
    (E)   Z originated in Sweden.

17. Exactly how many of the artifacts are there any one of which could have originated in Norway?

    (A)   one
    (B)   two
    (C)   three
    (D)   four
    (E)   five

18. Which one of the following CANNOT be true?

    (A)   Only V originated in Sweden.
    (B)   Only V and Z originated in Sweden.
    (C)   Only W and Y originated in Sweden.
    (D)   Only X and Z originated in Sweden.
    (E)   Only V, W, X, and Y originated in Sweden.

GO ON TO THE NEXT PAGE.

Questions 19–23

The employees of the Summit Company—J, K, L, and M—work a four-day workweek from Monday through Thursday. Every Monday, work begins on four raw workpieces, each of which is worked on for four consecutive days. On any given day, an employee works on exactly one workpiece. At the beginning of each workday after Monday, each workpiece is transferred from the employee who worked on it the previous day to another one of the employees, who will work on it that day. Workpieces cannot be transferred in any of the following ways:

From J to M
From K to J
From L to J

19. Which one of the following describes four transfers of workpieces that could all occur together at the beginning of a particular workday?

(A)   From J to K; from K to L; from L to M; from M to J

(B)   From J to K; from K to M; from L to K; from M to J

(C)   From J to L; from K to M; from L to J; from M to K

(D)   From J to L; from K to J; from L to M; from M to K

(E)   From J to M; from K to L; from L to K; from M to J

GO ON TO THE NEXT PAGE.

20. Which one of the following transfers must occur at the beginning of any workday that is not a Monday?

    (A) From J to K
    (B) From J to L
    (C) From K to L
    (D) From L to M
    (E) From M to J

21. If one workpiece is worked on by only two of the four employees in the course of an entire workweek, those two employees must be

    (A) J and K
    (B) J and L
    (C) K and L
    (D) K and M
    (E) L and M

22. If L works on the same workpiece both on Tuesday and on Thursday, which one of the following must be true about that workpiece?

    (A) J works on it on Monday.
    (B) K works on it on Monday.
    (C) M works on it on Monday.
    (D) J works on it on Wednesday.
    (E) K works on it on Wednesday.

23. Which one of the following could be true about Tuesday?

    (A) Transfers from J to K and from K to M occur.
    (B) Transfers from J to L and from L to M occur.
    (C) Transfers from J to M and from M to J occur.
    (D) Transfers from K to L and from L to K occur.
    (E) Transfers from K to L and from L to M occur.

S T O P

IF YOU FINISH BEFORE TIME IS CALLED, YOU MAY CHECK YOUR WORK ON THIS SECTION ONLY.
DO NOT WORK ON ANY OTHER SECTION IN THE TEST.

Acknowledgment is made to the following sources from which material has been adapted for use in this test booklet:

Kwame Anthony Appiah, "Whose Culture Is It?" ©2006 by NYREV, Inc.

Bruce Bower, "Brain Roots of Music Depreciation." ©2004 by Science Service, Inc.

Benjamin Freedman, "Equipoise and the Ethics of Clinical Research." ©1987 by the Massachusetts Medical Society.

Michael Parfit, "The Essential Elements of Fire." ©1996 by the National Geographic Society.

Jack Shafer, "Shut Your Loophole." ©2007 by Washingtonpost.Newsweek Interactive Co. LLC.

Wait for the supervisor's instructions before you open the page to the topic.
Please print and sign your name and write the date in the designated spaces below.
Time: 35 Minutes

General Directions

u will have 35 minutes in which to plan and write an essay on the topic inside. Read the topic and the accompanying directions carefully. u will probably find it best to spend a few minutes considering the topic and organizing your thoughts before you begin writing. In your essay, sure to develop your ideas fully, leaving time, if possible, to review what you have written. **Do not write on a topic other than the one ecified. Writing on a topic of your own choice is not acceptable.**

special knowledge is required or expected for this writing exercise. Law schools are interested in the reasoning, clarity, organization, guage usage, and writing mechanics displayed in your essay. How well you write is more important than how much you write.

nfine your essay to the blocked, lined area on the front and back of the separate Writing Sample Response Sheet. Only that area will be roduced for law schools. Be sure that your writing is legible.

Both this topic sheet and your response sheet must be turned in to the testing staff
before you leave the room.

Topic Code
122155

Print Your Full Name Here		
Last	First	M.I.

Date
/   /

Sign Your Name Here

Scratch Paper
Do not write your essay in this space.

LSAT® Writing Sample Topic

Directions: The scenario presented below describes two choices, either one of which can be supported on the basis of the information given. Your essay should consider both choices and argue for one over the other, based on the two specified criteria and the facts provided. There is no "right" or "wrong" choice: a reasonable argument can be made for either.

A successful and politically active lawyer is deciding between two career moves: either to accept an appointment as a judge in the regional courts, or to run, with support from a major party, for a seat in the national legislature. Using the facts below, write an essay in which you argue for one choice over the other based on the following two criteria:

- The lawyer wants to have a significant impact on public policy and the future of the country.
- The lawyer wants to maintain a close-knit and prosperous family.

The judicial appointment is a permanent position. Regional judges are rarely removed from office. The regional courts decide at most one or two cases of wide significance in a year. A few regional judges advance to positions in the national courts where most significant cases are decided. Regional judges train law clerks, many of whom go on to important positions in public life. Judges work regular hours and are not required to travel. Judges have personal contact with important figures in government and business. Judges rarely have success in seeking other political office.

The legislative seat is in a highly competitive district and the holder faces frequent elections. New legislators seldom have much effect on legislation or government policy. Successful long-time legislators can greatly affect government policies and programs. The legislature is in session 36 weeks of the year. Legislators spend many hours campaigning and fundraising. They travel frequently between the national capital and their district. The national capital is a short flight from the lawyer's legislative district. Legislators are widely known in their districts and some eventually gain national recognition. A close and supportive family is a strong asset in politics.

WP-V12

Scratch Paper
Do not write your essay in this space.

Writing Sample Response Sheet

DO NOT WRITE
IN THIS SPACE

**Begin your essay in the lined area below.
Continue on the back if you need more space.**

Directions:

1. Use the Answer Key on the next page to check your answers.

2. Use the Scoring Worksheet below to compute your raw score.

3. Use the Score Conversion Chart to convert your raw score into the 120–180 scale.

Scoring Worksheet

1. Enter the number of questions you answered correctly in each section.

	Number Correct
SECTION I.................	_____
SECTION II................	_____
SECTION III..............	_____
SECTION IV	_____

2. Enter the sum here: _____
   This is your Raw Score.

Conversion Chart
For Converting Raw Score to the 120–180 LSAT Scaled Score
LSAT Form 5LSN113

Reported Score	Raw Score Lowest	Raw Score Highest
180	99	101
179	98	98
178	97	97
177	96	96
176	95	95
175	94	94
174	93	93
173	92	92
172	90	91
171	89	89
170	88	88
169	87	87
168	85	86
167	84	84
166	82	83
165	81	81
164	79	80
163	77	78
162	76	76
161	74	75
160	72	73
159	71	71
158	69	70
157	67	68
156	65	66
155	64	64
154	62	63
153	60	61
152	58	59
151	56	57
150	55	55
149	53	54
148	51	52
147	49	50
146	48	48
145	46	47
144	44	45
143	43	43
142	41	42
141	39	40
140	38	38
139	36	37
138	35	35
137	33	34
136	32	32
135	30	31
134	29	29
133	28	28
132	26	27
131	25	25
130	24	24
129	23	23
128	22	22
127	21	21
126	20	20
125	19	19
124	18	18
123	17	17
122	16	16
121	15	15
120	0	14

ANSWER KEY

SECTION I

1.	D	8.	B	15.	D	22.	C
2.	E	9.	C	16.	C	23.	E
3.	C	10.	A	17.	D	24.	D
4.	A	11.	C	18.	D	25.	D
5.	B	12.	D	19.	A	26.	B
6.	D	13.	B	20.	C	27.	B
7.	B	14.	B	21.	A		

SECTION II

1.	D	8.	D	15.	D	22.	C
2.	C	9.	D	16.	D	23.	A
3.	B	10.	C	17.	B	24.	A
4.	A	11.	C	18.	E	25.	B
5.	E	12.	E	19.	C	26.	D
6.	C	13.	C	20.	B		
7.	E	14.	C	21.	B		

SECTION III

1.	C	8.	A	15.	B	22.	E
2.	B	9.	E	16.	D	23.	C
3.	D	10.	D	17.	D	24.	A
4.	E	11.	A	18.	C	25.	D
5.	C	12.	C	19.	D		
6.	C	13.	C	20.	B		
7.	A	14.	B	21.	E		

SECTION IV

1.	B	8.	C	15.	E	22.	E
2.	E	9.	D	16.	A	23.	E
3.	B	10.	A	17.	C		
4.	D	11.	E	18.	C		
5.	A	12.	B	19.	A		
6.	E	13.	B	20.	E		
7.	E	14.	A	21.	C